**THE**  **)**

*Published in the same series by Pan Books*

The PGA European Tour Guide to Better Golf
The LTA Guide to Better Tennis
The British Ski Federation Guide to Better Skiing
The AAA Guide to Better Athletics
The ASA Guide to Better Swimming
The SRA/WSRA Guide to Better Squash
The KUGB Guide to Better Karate

# THE NEIL ADAMS
# GUIDE TO BETTER
# JUDO

**NEIL ADAMS MBE**

*Photographs by Dave Finch*

*A Pan Original*

**Pan Books**
**London, Sydney and Auckland**

# Contents

# *Foreword*

Judo is a sport which makes particular demands on those aiming for the highest success. All the physical qualities are required to a high degree. In addition, a tough indomitable spirit must complement the physical abilities. Beyond this is another dimension – the technical one. A judo fighter may have a good fighting spirit and be supremely fit, yet without skilful technique he would be like a man trying to batter down a door; technique is the key that opens the door.

The author of this book, Neil Adams MBE, is remarkable in that he has all the above qualities. He is renowned in the judo world as a technician and fighter and his record as World Champion and Olympic silver medallist proves this. Not only does this book give the soundest advice on technique and training, it also gives an insight into the author's mentality and approach to judo. Neil Adams has called upon a vast knowledge of judo skills, including not only his own but those of many of the world's top competitors, whose special techniques and training methods are recorded here.

It has been said that there are many paths to the top. Neil's particular one has been marked by his burning determination, razor-sharp throws and unstoppable groundwork. The young up-and-coming competitor, or anyone with an interest in judo, will find this extremely interesting and beneficial reading.

It has been my fortune to have had close contact with Neil both on and off the mat over a number of years and I can confidently recommend his book to all aspiring judoka.

Syd Hoare 7th Dan
Chairman of the British Judo Association
1985–87

# Introduction

Judo is without a doubt one of the toughest physical contact sports in the world today. It requires tremendous endurance, skill and power, as well as a neverending list of techniques to be mastered. Recognized as an Olympic sport in 1964, it is the safest of the fighting sports, attracting people of all ages from seven years to seventy.

I started when I was seven, encouraged by my father, who to this day still remains the greatest influence on my judo career. He was my coach until I was sixteen and handled my early training very carefully, which is one of the reasons why my interest has never waned. Noticing my ability, he decided that I needed a bigger club at which to develop my skills, so at the age of ten I went to Coventry Judo Club and remained there for the duration of my junior career. When I was sixteen my father decided that London was the only place for me to further myself, and sent me down to train with such judoka as Brian Jacks (Senior European Champion in 1970 and 1973, world bronze medallist 1968, Olympic bronze medallist 1972), David Starbrook (nine times British Open Champion, Olympic bronze medallist 1976, world bronze medallist 1973 and

1975) and Keith Remfrey (Olympic silver medallist 1976), all of whom were Olympic medallists I had hero-worshipped since I was a young boy.

In 1974 I was to win the Espoir (young men's) European Championships, which began my thirteen-year international career. In 1976 I won my first British Open Senior medal, losing narrowly to Vass Morrison (British Open Champion also in 1972, '73 and '77), in the final. It was Vass who was to take the only Olympic place at my weight in Montreal. Bitterly disappointed, I realized that my training had to be structured in a much more professional manner and I began 1977 with my ambitions and aims clearly defined.

I first encountered Cyril Carter, a former gymnast, at the 1976 British Open, and after meeting on several occasions we started to put together a structured training programme. Cyril has degrees in Physical Education, Sports Physiology and Psychology, and the vast experience of a past competitive gymnastic career – these were the strengths of my coach and companion. This was one of the first times that any British judo fighter had associated with an individual on a one-to-one basis (although I did use other coaches as well).

9

It was something that the Eastern bloc countries had been doing for decades. Unfortunately, in many sports in Great Britain we still have the true amateur British system, the good old 'get up and have a go'. It is only the individuals who are adopting the professional approach necessary to reach the top, with only a handful of capable coaches to call on.

Two of my biggest problems in the early days were overtraining and losing weight, which often resulted in illness. By 1977 my natural weight was about 74 kg and I was still opting for the light-welterweight class of under 71 kg. It was at this time that I should have been thinking of going into the next category of light middleweight – under 78 kg – in preparation for the 1980 Olympic Games. In fact three years later I was still dropping to the under 71 kg category, although sometimes fighting at the higher weight with success. This mistake probably cost me one of my gold medals in the Olympic Games.

At the European Junior Championships I was to meet a man in the final whom I would fight many times over the following years: Ezio Gamba of Italy (1979 World silver medallist, 1980 Olympic Champion, 1982 European Champion). A close but decisive victory now brought me my second intermediate-level European Championship, this time in the under twenty-ones. This year also saw my big breakthrough into the senior ranks, winning the first of my eight British Open titles, beating the experienced Ronnie Nilsson of Sweden in the final.

In May of that year, 1977, I was to have the biggest test of my career so far, at the European Senior Championships in Helsinki. After fighting some very hard bouts all day, I eventually reached the semifinal stage, facing the formidable, and probably best light welterweight of all time, the Russian 1975 World and 1976 Olympic Champion, Vladimir Nevzerov. At eighteen years of age and hungry for success it really did not matter who was facing me – I just wanted to win! I remember the casual way in which Nevzerov treated his young opponent, and then the surprise when he realized that he'd have to pull out all the stops to win. The fact that he only just won, and that I was disappointed, meant that the bronze medal I eventually won was not good enough for me. I fought him again two days later in the team competition and was treated this time with slightly more respect. I lost again and the contest was as close as the first, but of course I was still not happy at the prospect of losing, even to Nevzerov. I was never to fight Nevzerov again as he retired soon after, remaining one of the all-time great judoka.

My year for learning was 1978. I lost the final of the British Open Championships, at the higher weight of under 78 kg, to Jean-Pierre Gilbert of France by a submission strangle that no one, including myself, had ever seen before. It was a strangle that was later to win me many contests. This was the turning point in my career; I decided that my groundwork was not up to standard. After months of study and hard perseverance, a change in my judo became apparent and my armoury was increasing all the time.

In the 1978 European Championships in Ludwigshafen I once again dropped weight to under 71 kg, and was to be robbed of my very first European Senior title because of extremely poor refereeing at the semifinal stage against the enormously experienced Gunther Kruger of East Germany, (1974 and 1978 European Champion). I had won my second Senior European bronze, but still had to break the barrier into the senior ranks. The stage was now set and I knew that with good training and a little bit of good luck I would reach my goal.

In 1979 I once again dropped my weight to under 71 kg and was desperate to avenge my previous defeat in the British Open Championships. This I did, and I was now looking forward to the European Championships in May. Everything went according to plan, beating Kruger in the semifinals and avenging the referee's mistake from the previous year. In the finals I met my old adversary, Ezio Gamba, and after two minutes scored the winning throw, which at the final bell gave me the first of my European Senior Championships wins. I was now extremely confident that I could win the World Championships in Paris – little did I know that Gamba would be the man to stop me. After a very tough draw, including Velujevic of Yugoslavia, Talaj of Poland and Kruger, and some very convincing wins, I once again faced Gamba, this time for a place in the World Championships final. I was knocked down by Gamba in the early seconds and although I fought for my life for the remainder of the contest, I narrowly missed being the first British man to reach any world final. This meant that I was to fight Christian Dyot of France (1977 Junior French Champion, and 1979 and 1982 French Champion) for the bronze and, after what I can only describe as a war, managed to win my first Senior world medal.

It was apparent now that the amount of weight I was losing before each event was taking its toll, especially in the latter part of the competition. My problem was to decide at which weight I would compete in the 1980 Moscow Olympics. I was once again undecided, and contested the British Open in the higher weight. This time I was successful and I felt that at last I was getting used to my heavier opponents. The irony is that at the European Championships later that year my weight was the lowest that it had been for some time, probably because of the heavy training schedule I had been following prior to the event. Obviously outmatched by my opponents' strength during the competition, I was resorting to my competition experience, extra speed and contest strategy to win through each round. In the final I faced Harald Heinke of East Germany, (1979 World bronze medallist and 1980 Olympic bronze medallist) previously 1978 and 1979 European Champion at 78 kg, and probably one of the biggest and strongest of the middleweight class. I think that I fought the best tactical match of my life that day, springing on to his back at every opportunity for an armlock (submission). Although I did not have the power to straighten his arm, at the end of the contest I had won my second European title with a unanimous decision on tactical grounds, with a rather disgruntled Heinke walking off the mat wondering whether he had been in a fight or not! So yet again it was clear that judo was not just a fighting sport but a strategic game to be studied at all levels.

Just before the Olympics I decided to drop down to my old weight, and it was the hardest weight loss that I had ever endured. My body was accepting the extra weight and was stabilizing at about 75 kg. I now realize that it is impossible to drop great amounts of weight, unless of course you are vastly overweight. Ideally you should be training within two kilos of your fighting weight. In the Moscow Olympics I lost too much weight and suffered the consequences. The loss of the final by a decision was a great disappointment to me, and of course I then decided to push my weight up to the higher category of 78 kg permanently. The following year was probably the greatest of my judo career, beating the Japanese Jiro Kase in the final of the World Championships by an armlock. At last I was crowned World Champion.

When I defended the World title two years later, I was probably in better shape than ever before. In fact I lost the final to Hikage of Japan (also World Champion in 1985) by what I thought was a controversial decision – I felt that I had done enough for my second World title.

After these championships it was getting more and more difficult to motivate myself. Two more European titles followed in 1983–84 and I was now looking forward to my second Olympic Games in Los Angeles. Although I knew that my physical condition in the Olympics was very good, I was finding it increasingly difficult to apply myself mentally.

The Olympic Games is the one event in the world that you can never predict, and no one could have seen that the only time in my life when I was ever to be thrown for ippon would be in the final of the 1984 Olympic Games in Los Angeles. After beating the most difficult people in the competition and leading the final against the relatively unknown Frank Wienecke of West Germany, (who was to become European Champion in 1986) I was caught with the judo version of a lucky punch that was to deprive me yet again of an Olympic title. This was to be my last event, but I decided that I was not going to finish on a bad result.

1985 was supposed, at one time, to be my last year of competition, and in the European Championships I won with probably one of my best performances ever. This form was a great contrast to my performance later that year in the World Championships, where I lost once again to Hikage of Japan, this time on a penalty. I just managed to get a bronze medal on a day that never went well for me from the start. I felt this really must be my last competition, and I was looking forward to a well-earned rest in 1986.

I had reached the stage in my career where it was difficult to enjoy what I was doing, and I realized that adjustments to my training were badly needed. However, I am now very relaxed, both mentally and physically, and am enjoying my judo more than ever before – so much so that after two years' rest I am refreshed and ready to start competing again! But being a competition judoka is really only a part of judo in general, and I hope that the pages which follow will help you with your sport, no matter what your aims are.

Everyone has to begin somewhere, but cultural differences all over the world make it a lot harder for someone living in Belgium, for example, with only 20,000 practising judoka, than for someone living in Japan with 2.5 million people practising judo. However, the sacrifices are the same and it takes many years of study and hard work to reach world-class level. Not everyone wants to reach such heights, and one of the beauties of the sport is the assortment of people from all walks of life practising judo for totally different reasons.

This is a unique book, with international champions, all of world-class status, giving you the benefit of their years of experience, from the very beginnings to the pinnacles of their careers. The importance of laying a good foundation cannot be overemphasized, for it is often bad teaching early on that results in technical errors later.

There is one chapter (page 25) on the basic principles that make up the sport, including essential information on using hands, body and legs. It is probably one of the most important chapters and you should study it carefully, but understand that every person will carry out a technique in a different way because of size, stature and ability. The basic principles remain the same whatever the technique, and should be used in both tachi-waza (standing practice) and ne-waza (groundwork practice).

New techniques and new variations can be learnt as you progress with your judo. Try to find a partner equally as keen as yourself to work within the roles of both tori (attacker) and uke (defender). Each is as important as the other. A good uke usually makes a good tori, so you should try to perfect both.

In this book I have given specific training routines for the very keen judoka, such as special uchi-komi (repetition) programmes which are important for ingraining techniques. Also included is advice on physical conditioning, which is important in such a physical sport. The better the condition you are in, the easier it is to train longer and harder.

It must be noted that in translating the terminology, it is impossible to give exact meanings for some Japanese terms, as they are often poetically descriptive. Please also remember that although it is not easy to learn from a photograph, you can experiment and develop your own particular way of performing these techniques from the explanations I have given. One of the best ways to use this book is as a companion to your training in the dojo (training hall). It is a guide for you, no matter what you wish to achieve in judo. In the end you only get out of the sport what you put in.

Work hard and enjoy your judo and remember Dr Jigoro Kano's philosophy:

'Judo is an education for life.'

# The history of judo

It was because of one man and a dream that judo is today recognized as the safest fighting Olympic sport.

Jigoro Kano, born in 1860, was the founder of judo as we know it today. He graduated from the Tokyo Imperial University with a degree in Literature and one year later gained another degree in Philosophy. Kano was a prominent figure in the Japanese Olympic movement following the revival of the Games in 1896, and although judo was not admitted until 1964, he was able to get judo accepted into the Japanese education system. As the head of education for the Ministry of Education he used his influence to establish judo in its own right.

As a young man Kano studied the Tenshin Shinyo Jyu style of ju-jitsu under Fukudo and Iso, both instructors of the famous Komu Sho central martial arts college. The origins of ju-jitsu are uncertain, and there are several different theories. Many think that it was brought over from China in the 1660s, although this story never convinced Kano. It was a little later that he was to clarify his own analysis of ju-jitsu and relate it to his own style. This was the birth of Jigoro Kano's judo, known as Kodokan Judo.

Although ju-jitsu and judo were similar,

Opposite: *The pull over or side throw, the beginning of the modern tai-otoshi*
Above: *Jigoro Kano, the father of modern judo*

ju-jitsu with its joint locks, throws and striking with hands, feet and elbows could be brutal, even deadly. The advantage of Kodokan Judo was that it could be practised with control and thus far less danger.

In 1873 the Japanese government brought the existing samurai class to an end. The wearing of swords in public places was forbidden, and therefore the possibility of confrontations which often ended in death was eradicated. This caused the samurai to split into two opposing groups, many joining the police and able to wear their swords on duty, and the others becoming a form of resistance trying to restore the ancient samurai class. The government eventually managed to suppress the latter.

The government started to look for a form of hand-to-hand fighting which could be taught in military academies all over Japan. Ju-jitsu or Kodokan Judo were the two obvious choices. In 1886 a special match was arranged between fifteen top ju-jitsu fighters and fifteen top judoka, resulting in a win for Kano's judo and its acceptance as a government-approved sport. Later, Kodokan Judo was approved and accepted into schools and colleges as part of the educational system in Japan.

In judo's early days women were practising, although at the time Jigoro Kano was not sure what their future role would be. It was eleven years after the founding of Kano's judo that he began to instruct a group of women led by Kayatani Sueko. For the first month they practised only ju-no-kata (the forms of gentleness, or simple kata) and for the second month only ukemi (breakfalls). In 1923 the

*Yukio Tani* (left), *the founder of British judo*

instruction of women started officially at the Kodokan (the first judo school in Japan) and they practised kata, (traditional sequences of movement that act as a training drill), light randori (free fighting practice), technique training and self-defence.

Kano felt that women should not do hard randori training or competition judo and it was not until 1933 that a woman, Kozaki Kanika, was promoted to 1st dan. To distinguish between men's and women's grades a white stripe ran down the middle of the women's belt. This is not used today. It was only when judo moved to Europe in the 1930s that the possibility of women training in the same way as men became reality.

Judo arrived in Britain at the turn of the century, and Yukio Tani was among a number of Japanese whose job was to advertise judo. Tani travelled all over the country demonstrating his skills at music halls and taking on any challengers.

*Gunji Koizumi, the founder of The Budokwai*

Finally, when all the other Japanese judoka had gone home, Tani stayed and was appointed chief instructor at a new club in England called The Budokwai. Neither Tani nor the club's founder, Gunji Koizumi, could have possibly known that The Budokwai was to become the most famous judo school outside Japan and the first in Europe.

Koizumi was to European judo what Kano was to world judo and it was in July 1948 that the British Judo Association was formed. Four days later, under the chairmanship of Trevor Leggett, the constitution of a European Judo Union was approved. Three years later, the International Judo Federation was formed as an international intercontinental body.

During the war, all judo instructors in Japan were ordered to teach unarmed combat to the troops. This was prohibited when occupation forces arrived and all martial arts taught in schools and public institutions were banned. The ban was officially lifted in 1951 and Kodokan Judo was reborn. In 1949 judo was united into one organization under the presidency of Resei Kano, the only son of Jigoro Kano.

American involvement in judo started just after the war when Theodore Roosevelt's interest in the sport resulted in the Japanese sending a highly ranked judoka over to America to give him private lessons. However, it was some time before America gained her first black belt. It was the women, not the men, who led the way in to top world-class competition some years later.

Prior to the introduction of judo into the Olympic Games in 1964, the major event in the judo calendar was the World Championships, which were inaugurated in 1956 and held every other year. The first Championships, held in Japan, were fought at open weight, which meant that there were no weight categories.

In 1961, a giant Dutchman called Anton Geesink (who also claimed the European

*Olympic and World Champion Yasuhiro Yamashita (Japan); Olympic gold medallist Anton Geesink (Holland)*

Championship fifteen times, as well as becoming World Champion again in 1965) became the first man to break the consistent domination of the Japanese by beating the World Champion, Sone. In 1964 he repeated this victory against the Japanese and became not only an Olympic champion but a judo legend. It was at these Olympics that weight categories were introduced for international competition, and this meant that judo was not just a sport for the giants. Three categories were formed in addition to the open weight. These were: Lightweight (U67.5 kg), Middleweight (U80 kg) and Heavyweight (O80 kg).

The inclusion of judo in the Olympic movement was a real boost for judo as a worldwide sport, and more and more countries began to start training judoka in a more professional manner. After all, if they were to beat the Japanese they had to train like them.

The newest and most dynamic country to enter the judo scene was the Soviet Union, who in 1962 took a team to the European Championships which managed to win five medals, even though it was their first competition. They had done so well because of the influence of sambo wrestling, a national sport in the Soviet Union since the 1930s. Sambo wrestling is a mixture of Graeco-Roman wrestling, Turkish wrestling and judo, incorporating many ju-jitsu movements. The word 'sambo' in Russian means 'self-defence', and it is thought that this form of wrestling derived from the Russian Anatoly Kharlampie and some of his associates, who were studying different forms of wrestling and self-defence, including

judo, in the 1930s. During the 1960s the Russians revolutionized modern judo with their unorthodox judo techniques, and along with Geesink they made people realize that maybe the Japanese could be beaten at their own game.

In 1966 it was decided to increase the number of weight categories to five with an additional open weight. These categories were: Lightweight (U63 kg), Light middleweight (U70 kg), Middleweight (U80 kg), Light heavyweight (U90 kg) and Heavyweight (O90 kg).

In the 1967 World Championships in Salt Lake City yet another Dutchman, Wilhelm Ruska (six times European Champion, twice Olympic Champion, World silver medallist in 1969), broke the Japanese domination by winning the heavyweight category. However, two years later in 1971 the Japanese once again reigned supreme by winning all five weight categories plus the open weight, although all other medals were won by European fighters.

In 1972 Ruska created judo history by winning both the heavyweight and the open weight Olympic titles, and the Russian Chochoshvili by winning the light heavyweight title. (Shota Chochoshvili also won the World bronze medal in 1975.)

The Japanese were once again forced to realize the potential of the rest of the world as, one by one, their domination of each weight category was being broken.

In 1974 it was decided that if women's judo was successfully conducted by at least three continental unions, the International Judo Union would consider sponsoring a first World Championships.

Following a trial competition that year an annual European Championships for women was established. In Britain, the first Women's British Open was held in 1971 and attracted fighters from West Germany. It was also watched by observers from the Netherlands. It is now an annual event drawing women judoka from all over the world.

The Eastern bloc countries were at first reluctant to enter women for international competitions, probably because they were not making such rapid progress as in the West. They had been restricted to practising in their own countries, while Western women were constantly meeting other international judoka to train and compete with. If they were to catch up, they realized they had to send teams abroad. Poland was one of the first of these countries to enter teams for international matches, and although at the beginning they were relatively weak and easily beaten by Western judoka, this encouraged more socialist countries to enter their own teams. The supremacy of the British, West German, French and Austrian women was now under threat and it was only a matter of time before Eastern bloc countries began catching up. This of course can only add to the rapid improvement that women's judo has shown over the last fifteen years.

The first Pan American women's judo tournament was held in 1977 and was largely dominated by the American team which had been competing internationally for some time. In 1980 the first Women's World Championships were held in New York and since then they have been held bi-annually. In 1988 women's judo will be an exhibition sport in the Olympic Games and in 1992 it will be fully recognized as part of the Olympic movement.

The Japanese have been slow to accept that women's judo is here to stay. Although their women have been technically very good they have lacked contest experience in the past, resulting in only one bronze medal at the first World Championships. However, that attitude is changing and the standard of the Japanese team is rapidly catching up with the rest of the world. They won their first World title in 1982 and look set to win many more in the near future.

In men's judo the Japanese no longer lead exclusively, and World and Olympic titles have been changing hands between judoka from all over the world since 1972. Even countries that twenty years ago were considered an easy passage into the next round are producing World and Olympic champions. It seems they are winning despite their sometimes poor judo systems, proving that if you want to win badly enough, you can do it! However, with the emergence of South Korea as a judo force equal to Japan, and the rapid improvement of all participating judo countries around the world, it indicates that a professionally run squad system is what is needed in most countries.

With men's and women's judo progressing all the time, who knows where it will go next. I look forward to finding out. My only hope is that judo is not just thought of as an Olympic sport, for with our long and illustrious history, and the fact that for many, judo becomes a lifestyle and an art, we will always be much more than 'just' a sport!

# The grading system

For many judoka the grading system acts as a form of motivation. To reach the highest possible grade becomes the principle aim. It originated from the Japanese system used in all the indigenous arts and crafts, ranging from chess and flower arranging to fencing and judo. In Japan the grading system is an indication of status, although it also acts as a motivation for improving skills.

It is a shame that in many countries today the system can be abused in order to make money from judoka, and thus loses its full original purpose.

## SENIORS

In every country the grading system has a different structure which is constantly changing. For example, in Japan they have only three kyu (coloured belt) grades before advancing to the dan (black belt) grades. In Great Britain, fifteen is the age at which you can first obtain a senior grade. There are nine kyu grades to be achieved before commencing the dan grades. They start with the white belt and progress as follows:

| | |
|---|---|
| 9th kyu | = yellow belt |
| 8th kyu/7th kyu | = orange belt |
| 6th kyu/5th kyu | = green belt |
| 4th kyu/3rd kyu | = blue belt |
| 2nd kyu/1st kyu | = brown belt |

Only when you are a 1st kyu standard can you begin to collect points for your 1st dan. One hundred points are needed and these can only be accumulated at specific point-scoring competitions that are approved by the governing body or by an official judo grading. Having acquired 100 points, you can then take the theory examination. It is possible to take a short cut to obtaining the 1st dan by winning two preliminary fights at a grading, one by ippon (one point, score value of ten points) and one by waza-ari, but both against 1st kyus. This then qualifies the judoka for a line-up of three people (all 1st kyu) and all have to be beaten by an ippon score in order to qualify for the theory examination.

The theory examination varies, but may consist of a demonstration of technique followed by some of the kata. The examination becomes harder the higher the dan grades progress.

The standard of the kyu grades and 1st dans in each country can vary enormously. In Japan most of the children in high school from the ages of fourteen to sixteen are 1st dans, but in other countries the age can be much higher. However, within the dan system these differences normally even out from the 2nd dan upwards. I would say that throughout the world the dan grades from 3rd dan are quite universal in standard.

It is interesting to note that there are no weight categories when a judoka fights for the belts at a grading. This means that someone of 60 kg may have to fight someone of 100 kg. However, men and women are graded separately.

Usually the highest competitive dan grade is a 5th dan, although there have been one or two competing 6th dans. After the 5th dan has been achieved the grades are then awarded for contributions towards the sport in terms of knowledge and service.

The 10th dan is the highest dan ever to have been achieved by a judoka, although it is written that a 12th dan is possible. The dan grade belt system is as follows:

| | |
|---|---|
| 1st dan | = black belt |
| 2nd dan | = black belt |
| 3rd dan | = black belt |
| 4th dan | = black belt |
| 5th dan | = black belt |
| 6th dan | = red/white belt |
| 7th dan | = red/white belt |
| 8th dan | = red/white belt |
| 9th dan | = red belt |
| 10th dan | = red belt |

# JUNIORS

The junior grading system differs even more than the senior, with many clubs operating and creating their own systems for juniors. Often the instructor determines how he thinks his pupils should be graded.

In Japan there is no junior grading system and very few competitions for juniors between the ages of eight and fifteen. I think that something can be learned from this, as often there is too much emphasis on winning competitions rather than on learning and enjoying judo. However, competition has it benefits, and so a controlled competitive programme is important.

The coloured belt system is used in Great Britain and there are eighteen mons (junior grades) to be won. There are three standards to each coloured belt and these are indicated with red stripes around one end of the belt.

The mon grades are as follows:

| | |
|---|---|
| 1st mon | = white belt + one red stripe |
| 2nd mon | = white belt + two red stripes |
| 3rd mon | = white belt + three red stripes |
| 4th mon | = yellow belt + one red stripe |
| 5th mon | = yellow belt + two red stripes |
| 6th mon | = yellow belt + three red stripes |
| 7th mon | = orange belt + one red stripe |
| 8th mon | = orange belt + two red stripes |
| 9th mon | = orange belt + three red stripes |
| 10th mon | = green belt + one red stripe |
| 11th mon | = green belt + two red stripes |
| 12th mon | = green belt + three red stripes |
| 13th mon | = blue belt + one red stripe |
| 14th mon | = blue belt + two red stripes |
| 15th mon | = blue belt + three red stripes |
| 16th mon | = brown belt + one red stripe |
| 17th mon | = brown belt + two red stripes |
| 18th mon | = brown belt + three red stripes |

You don't have to work your way through every grade to qualify for entering senior gradings. If, at the age of fifteen, you have progressed to a coloured belt, you can then attempt the equivalent coloured belt in the senior grades. In Japan, however, the senior grading system is used with juniors from the age of about fourteen.

The grading system used for judo is unique to martial arts and is envied by many other sports. It is not only a measure of personal proficiency but is part of an original grading system used in Japan for centuries.

# The fundamentals

The teaching of good fundamentals is important for good judo and a judoka should understand exactly how and why they work. Once the fundamentals of a sport have been mastered, techniques begin to fall into place.

Differences in size and stature of judoka mean that although the fundamentals are the same, they have to be adapted to suit each individual. Ingrid Berghmans of Belgium – Women's World Champion in 1980, '82, '84 and '86, and European Champion in 1983, '85 and '86 – weighing 72 kg, and Karen Briggs of Great Britain, World Champion in 1982, '84 and '86, and European Champion 1982–87, weighing only 48 kg, are both at the top of their categories and both have excellent technical judo. Although they are physically very different they often use the same techniques successfully. So body makeup and shape play a large part in the way in which techniques are performed.

The three essential ingredients for any judo technique are the correct use of hands, body and legs. The main difficulty for the judoka is coordinating these to produce a continuous movement.

## HANDS

The hands are essential for all judo movements because they are used to start and finish the techniques. Kumikata (The method of grappling of two contestants) is so much a part of modern judo that a whole contest can elapse without a proper attack being made if judoka are unable to obtain a grip on their opponent's jacket in order to attack. Gripping techniques have become more skilled and complex nowadays. It is increasingly difficult to get a traditional, basic lapel and sleeve grip because of the corresponding development of skilled blocking techniques. This means that either a double lapel or a yama-arashi grip (a cross grip, as used in the 'mountain storm' throw) is having to be taken.

To start an attack in judo, you must break through your opponent's defences.

*1  Angelo Parisi of France demonstrates the double lapel grip*

Normally a judoka will use his or her arms to defend, so to overcome this barrier, place one or both of your hands inside your opponent's arms and create enough space for an attack by pushing your opponent's arms outwards. Because the opponent's defences have only been temporarily weakened, the technique must be performed immediately, and at speed.

Angelo Parisi of France (see photograph 1), Olympic Champion in Moscow, 1980, European Champion 1972, '73, '77, '83 and '84, is one of the few judoka in the world who favours a double lapel grip, because he is able to throw equally well on the left and on the right. This can be very confusing for his opponents, who cannot predict which direction he is going to attack from. A double lapel grip is very unusual but works well for Angelo as the traditional sleeve grip is not essential for his techniques. When using his double lapel grip, Angelo needs to maintain perfect control of his opponent in order to prevent the opponent from putting an arm down to stop an ippon from being scored. Angelo manages to keep this control by an extreme pulling action on his opponent's lapel as they are being thrown. In photograph 2, note how Angelo has turned his opponent in order to finish the attack and prevented his opponent from putting their hands down.

Karen Briggs favours a strong sleeve grip in order to throw her opponents. She chooses techniques which are performed at great speed and near to the ground. This strong sleeve grip enables Karen to throw her opponents on their backs.

Karen's tomoe-nage (stomach throw) is one of her best techniques and she per-

*2 Parisi maintains perfect control by an extreme pulling action on his opponent's lapels as he is being thrown*

forms it at immense speed and from varying directions, as, for example, in photograph 3. Here, Karen is throwing her opponent on the way to winning her first Commonwealth title in 1986. Note the very strong sleeve grip used to finish the technique.

*3 Karen Briggs using a tomoe-nage*

*4a, b, c, d Karen's low centre of gravity enables her to rotate her opponent near the ground. Note the extreme pulling action on the sleeve*

Karen also uses a very low tai-otoshi (body drop) which is again performed at speed – see photographs 4a, b, c, d. Her low centre of gravity enables the opponent to be rotated near to the ground. Without such a strong sleeve grip they would land on their face rather than their back. Tai-otoshi is also one of my favourite techniques, but with a yama-arashi grip. This cross grip can be very awkward for your opponent, especially if you are both right handed, as your hand prevents him or her from being able to turn inwards to throw you. This grip can also create problems for a left-handed judoka, although not with such a good effect.

*5a Demonstrating the yama-arashi grip*

*b Using it in competition*

As you can see in photographs 5a, b, I am using the yama-arashi grip on my opponent. It is not permitted to hold one side of the jacket with two hands without attacking immediately. I use this rule to my advantage and prefer to let my opponents try to grip my own sleeve. As they lunge forward, thus losing their balance, I catch their sleeve to throw them using a strong pulling action.

Ingrid Berghmans is one of the tallest women judoka in the world and uses her height to her advantage. Because she is taller than most of her opponents she prefers a very high collar grip (see photograph 6) in order to control their heads. Once Ingrid obtains this grip she almost always attacks with her strong uchi-mata (inner thigh throw) technique. (See Tachi-waza, page 45).

It is not always possible to obtain a favourite grip. Ingrid finds that many of her opponents try to avoid her dominating hand by keeping their shoulders away

from her. In order to get her high lapel grip Ingrid firstly has to catch her opponent's left arm with her left hand and pull it across her body enabling her to take hold of the jacket. Once this has been achieved, she then releases the left sleeve

*6 Ingrid Berghmans prefers a high collar grip*

*7a, b, c Ingrid demonstrating how she foils her opponent's attempts to avoid her collar grip*

and catches hold of the other sleeve in order to attack. This is illustrated in photographs 7a, b, c.

The heavier weights tend not to pluck at the jacket as much as the lighter weights in order to attack. Rather than constantly changing their grips like the lighter categories, they prefer to keep the same grip.

Yasuhiro Yamashita, who was World Champion 1979–83 and Olympic Champion in 1984, has a grip I would call the fundamental (kumikata) grip, holding the underside of his opponent's sleeve and a lapel at approximately shoulder height, as

*8 Yamashita demonstrating his traditional kumikata*

in photograph 8. This type of grip is perfect for his favourite technique, hopping uchi-mata, where he needs a strong pulling action on the sleeve and a pushing action against his opponent's head. It is by working these simultaneously that his technique is so dynamic and precise.

---

**TIP**

Try to be adventurous with your gripping skills and experiment with different grips for the same throws.

---

*9 The immobilization of an opponent's arms and head are vital with juji-gatame and sangaku-jime*

The hands are also very important for ne-waza techniques and like tachi-waza are used to begin an attack.

Juji-gatame (straight armlock) and sangaku-jime (triangular strangle) are two of the most favoured ne-waza techniques used in judo today. There are many variations of these techniques, but all begin with the control of the opponent's hands. As with tachi-waza, the opponent can make it very difficult to attack, but with juji-gatame and sangaku-jime it is vital that you begin the technique with the immobilization of the opponent's arms, photograph 9.

Note how Ingrid Berghmans, in photograph 10, has hooked her opponent's arm with her own right arm and has at the same time controlled their head. Ingrid could use her left arm equally as well to achieve the same effect, (see photograph 11). From this position she can either turn her opponent for a juji-gatame or sangaku-jime, or on to their back for an osae-komi-waza (hold-down).

*10, 11, 12 In all three situations Ingrid has controlled her opponents' arms and head*

Photograph 12 shows Ingrid holding her opponent with a very strong tate-shiho-gatame (vertical four quarters hold). In an osae-komi-waza the use of the hands is obviously very important, and here Ingrid has clasped her own hands together to strengthen the technique. She has total control of the opponent's head and upper body.

Karen Briggs is equally as good with her ne-waza as with her tachi-waza and favours techniques such as shime-waza (strangle), tate-shiho-gatame and yoko-shiho-gatame (side four quarters hold). She changes at immense speed from tachi-waza to ne-waza and needs to maintain control of her opponents throughout.

Karen often searches for a shime-waza using her hands to create an opening around the opponent's neck. Her hands, in a wedge shape, slide either side of the neck. Once the opening is made there are a number of possibilities for different techniques she can attempt.

Yasuhiro Yamashita is one of the few heavyweights with good ne-waza attacks against his opponents and has won many of his contests with koshi-jime (hip strangle). In photograph 13 against Reszko of Poland (1981 European Champion) in the final of the 1981 World Championships, Yasuhiro used his hands with great effect to secure this koshi-jime and was able to keep complete control of his opponent throughout.

*13 Yamashita securing a koshi-jime against Resko of Poland*

# BODY

After the hands have been used successfully to start an attack, the correct use of the body is obviously very important for the continuation of the technique. The points of bodily contact used for a technique depend on the size of the judoka and the technique he or she chooses. Not all techniques require bodily contact although the use of the body still plays an important part in deciding the direction of movement.

The correct use of the body is very difficult to teach as there are so many variations for each technique. It is almost like teaching someone to balance on a bicycle. The final adjustment has to come from within the person learning. Usually, you are able to feel whether you have good contact or not, but it is a good idea to have a coach to watch and correct your techniques as you go along.

Angelo Parisi is a good example of a judoka who uses complete bodily contact with his seoi-otoshi (a movement which is a mixture – shoulder throw and body drop) technique. In photograph 14 Angelo is attacking with his favourite technique and although his centre of gravity (belt

14 *Parisi uses complete body contact with his seoi-otoshi*

15 *And when attacking with osoto-gari*

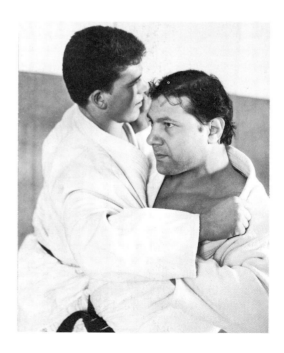

line) is lower than that of his opponent, he still has complete contact with the whole of his back against his opponent's front. His opponent is totally off-balance and Angelo would finish the throw by straightening his legs and pulling strongly with his hands to throw his opponent over his shoulders.

Angelo favours an osoto-gari (major outer reaping) attack and often links this with his seoi-otoshi. When his opponent resists the osoto-gari, Angelo changes the direction of the attack to the forward seoi-otoshi throw. He keeps body contact throughout the technique.

Photograph 15 shows Angelo attacking with osoto-gari. Notice the body contact he has and the way he is using his hands to pull his opponent towards him in order to obtain this contact. It is interesting to note that when Angelo uses the combination technique, he has body contact, firstly with his chest for the osoto-gari, and secondly with his back for the seoi-otoshi. To do this he has to completely change direction until the whole of his own back is in contact with his opponent's front (see photographs 16a and b).

*16a, b Parisi has body contact firstly with his chest for the osoto-gari, and then with his back for the seoi-otoshi*

*17 Ingrid throws her opponent with o-uchi-gari*

In photograph 17 you can see Ingrid Berghmans throwing her opponent with o-uchi-gari (major inner reaping). Note the chest contact and the strong pull she has on her opponent's collar in order to finish the technique. In this particular technique it can be dangerous to have your body side on to that of your opponent because of the possibility of being counterattacked. Therefore, for safety reasons it is important for Ingrid to have front contact with her opponent.

Ingrid uses her dominant grip to her advantage for her uchi-mata and pulls her opponent towards her to get the necessary contact. Photographs 18 and 19 show side and front views of Ingrid's uchi-mata. Notice the complete contact she has with her opponent's body and the way in which she has controlled their hands.

One of the most effective ways of using

*18, 19 Side and front views of Ingrid's uchi-mata*

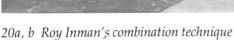

*20a, b Roy Inman's combination technique*

the body without actually having contact is with combination techniques. A combination technique is one in which a player can make an opponent think they are going to be thrown with one technique, but are actually thrown with another. This can be in the same or another direction. An example of a forward and backward combination is shown in photographs 20a, b, performed by Roy Inman, ex-British international and currently British women's team manager. Roy had a very successful combination technique. Using a strong uchi-mata throw to obtain resistance in the opposite direction, he was able to throw with kosoto-gari (minor outer reaping). His hands played a large part in making his opponent think that he was going one way, when he was in fact about to change direction halfway through the attack, allowing him to attack with another technique.

*21 Holding my opponent with mune-gatame*

The use of the body for ne-waza is just as important as for tachi-waza, and judoka should learn techniques with and without bodily contact. Full contact is essential in certain techniques, as is shown in photograph 21 where I am holding my opponent

35

*22a, b, c, d My opponent pushes against my chin to try to escape my osae-komi-waza*

with mune-gatame (chest hold) and have total chest contact and control of the opponent's head.

Total body contact can work to your opponent's advantage if you are fighting someone much stronger than yourself, as it is sometimes possible for them to turn you over and escape from your osae-komi-waza. This is why the use of the body in these techniques is so vital, as it must allow you constantly to adjust your own weight in order to maintain your osae-komi-waza against your opponent's vigorous movements.

In photographs 22a and b my opponent pushes against my chin to try to escape my osae-komi-waza. In photograph 22c I move my body to the side and then trap his arm by pulling it across his body – 22d. I then complete the movement by completely controlling my opponent's head by clasping my hands together. I maintain total body contact against his arm and chest to prevent his arm from moving.

Yasuhiro Yamashita is one of the few heavyweights to have a successful koshi-

jime. He uses his weight and power to his own advantage by trapping his opponent to the floor with his chest in order to prevent them from standing up. He then attacks with the koshi-jime.

One of the most difficult things to do in ne-waza is to turn an opponent from their front on to their back. This is where the use of the body is also very important, not only for attacking but also for defending, as there are many situations you might find yourself in during a contest.

If your opponent is on their front, there are a number of techniques to use which will turn them over incorporating the body, legs and arms. Most importantly, the opponent's head should be controlled as you make them turn. See in photographs 23a, b, c, d, how I am turning my opponent on to his back, and note control of the head and contact with the body.

*23a, b, c, d It is important to control your opponent as you turn them and go into an attacking position*

# LEGS

*24a, b, c, d  Ingrid demonstrates the use of the legs in her te-garuma counterattack*

The legs are the strongest individual part of the body and are not used to their full potential as often as they should be in judo. In both tachi-waza and ne-waza their use is vital to the techniques.

The lifting action of the legs is shown in photographs 24a, b, c, d. Here, Ingrid Berghmans is being attacked to the front with a harai-goshi (sweeping loin throw) attack. Notice the body contact she has with her opponent (photograph 24a) in order to control him fully. She now has a good posture for lifting, and has dropped her centre of balance (belt line) below her opponent's. In photographs 24b and c, Ingrid's left hand has passed between her opponent's legs; she has then straightened her legs and body in order to lift him up. To finish the technique (photograph 24d) she uses her body and hands to rotate her partner on to his back.

In photograph 25 Ingrid demonstrates a

*25 Ingrid demonstrates a fine example of tani-otoshi, this time driving her opponent backwards*

fine example of tani-otoshi (valley drop). She uses a backward driving action with her legs when she throws her partner.

The legs can also be used to hook, trap and sweep an opponent. With all these movements it is important to have good coordination of the legs.

26a, b  Demonstrating o-uchi-gari

## The hook

The o-uchi-gari in photographs 26a and b shows me transferring my opponent's weight with my hands on to the leg that I want to hook away. This is now his supporting leg and when it is taken away he falls to the mat.

## The sweep

In photograph 27 Angelo Parisi has swept his opponent's legs away with de-ashi-harai (advancing sweeping ankle). This is done when the opponent is moving sideways, therefore the leg coordination has to be perfectly timed in order to sweep the feet of his moving opponent from underneath him. Most sweeping actions require the sweeping leg to be as straight as possible.

27  Parisi sweeps his opponent's legs away with de-ashi-harai

# The trap

Yamashita's tai-otoshi clearly shows the importance of trapping his opponent's leg. With his strong hand action, and his efforts to stop his opponent from stepping forward, the player rotates on to his back, see photograph 28.

The legs also help to direct a throw and this can be seen in photograph 29 in this two-footed tomoe-nage attack by Karen Briggs on the Scottish champion, Ann-Marie Mulholland, in the final of the 1986 Commonwealth Games tournament. Her original attack was a one-footed yoko-(side) tomoe-nage at the edge of the competition area.

29 Below: *Karen Briggs with her favourite osae-komi-waza*

28 Above: *Yamashita's tai-otoshi. Note how he's trapped his opponent's left leg*

The legs are just as important for ne-waza techniques as they are for tachi-waza. A judoka with strong legs, such as Karen, can be extremely difficult to attack on the ground and often uses this strength to their own advantage.

I frequently use my legs to turn an opponent's attack to my advantage. This series of pictures shows me trapping my opponent's legs with my own (30a), and by controlling his head (30b), turning him over into a strong tate-shiho-gatame (30c).

Another excellent example of leg control and strength is shown in photographs 31a, b, of Ingrid Berghmans using the popular juji-gatame. She has control of her opponent by crossing her feet and using her legs to stop him from sitting up. Ingrid finally pulls his arms out to apply the kansetsu-waza (armlock).

Although the three parts of the body which make up the judo fundamentals have been described and explained separately, it is the judoka with the ability to combine and coordinate them who produces excellent techniques.

*30a, b, c* Left: *Using my legs to turn an opponent's attack to my advantage*
*31a, b* Right: *Ingrid Berghmans with another excellent example of leg control and strength using juji-gatame*

# Tachi-waza – standing techniques

When studying technique of any kind, it is important to keep an open mind. I have always maintained that two techniques are never performed identically, although they may contain certain similarities. The basic aims, though, do remain the same, and you should refer to the Fundamentals chapter and make sure that you fully understand them.

Not everyone will perform a technique beautifully, but everyone can still be very effective and achieve their objective.

In this chapter I will explain the differences in certain techniques when performed by fighters of varying statures. Remember that your method will contain your own style and may look a little different from the example that you see.

You are normally able to feel whether a technique works – your hands, body and legs move simultaneously in a reflex action which happens so quickly that you are unable to remember exactly what you have done. This reflex action is achieved through ingraining, which I have covered in the uchi-komi (repetition) section on page 93.

In this chapter I have taken a few of the most popular throws from the Gokyo (the forty basic tachi-waza/throwing techniques). All the throws I have chosen work well in competition.

## UCHI-MATA – INNER THIGH THROW

There are many variations of uchi-mata performed by world-class judoka. I have started with two of Yasuhiro Yamashita's variations.

# Yasuhiro Yamashita – o-uchi-gari

Yasuhiro has an extremely fast and effective o-uchi-gari. If his opponent has a strong resistance to this throw and successfully defends it, Yasuhiro has two options. The first is shown in sequence 1a, b, c, d. In 1a, he has attacked with his o-uchi-gari and at this stage looks quite strong. In 1b, his opponent has lifted his leg into the air to avoid it being swept away and is strongly resisting the rear attack. At this point Yasuhiro has decided to change the direction of the throw and uses his fantastic pulling action with his hands to pull his opponent's shoulder right the way round in order to make him lose his balance. In 1c, Yasuhiro uses his right leg to hop until (1d) his opponent cartwheels over his supporting leg, almost

*1a*

*b*

*c*

*d*

making the throw an uchi-mata.

Although it is difficult to illustrate the hop in a picture sequence, I can tell you that he has been known to start the technique on one edge of the contest area and, after six or seven hops, eventually finish in the other corner of the mat. The big advantage of this particular style of uchi-mata is that it can be done very successfully on tall opponents because the hopping action requires little body contact.

> **YAMASHITA'S TIP**
>
> The leg hopping and extreme pulling with the hands are the key to this technique.

Yasuhiro has a second variation that follows on from the first, in case his opponent is especially flexible and manages to defend against the first attack. If Yasuhiro decides that it will be difficult to cartwheel his opponent over, he changes his direction completely, this time throwing his opponent to the front. He once again uses the hopping action on his right leg, but his right foot changes direction and faces the direction in which he is about to throw his opponent. To finish the throw he straightens his right leg and extends on to his toes, which elevates his opponent on to his back.

# *Ingrid Berghmans*

As I mentioned earlier in the Fundamentals chapter, Ingrid is tall and prefers a high collar grip on her opponent's jacket. She uses this strong grip to her advantage because the opponent is now forced to

advance with the legs, giving Ingrid the hip contact she requires for the technique.

Photographs 2a and b show how she has made the opponent advance with one foot and 2c shows that her hips are now in line

*2a, b Ingrid Berghmans using her high collar grip . . .*

ready for contact prior to the throw. At this point the use of the leg is very important as Ingrid swings it backwards against her opponent's inner left thigh in order to lift them and rotate them on to their back: 2d, e.

---

**TIP**

The pulling action on the collar is very important to start your partner stepping forward. To complete the throw, the attacker should pull an opponent's arm downwards and across his chest, thus rotating them on to their back.

---

*c, d, e . . . in order to carry out her favourite uchi-mata throw*

# Brian Jacks – spinning uchi-mata

For a spinning uchi-mata it is important that you fully commit yourself by throwing your whole body into the technique. To catch your opponent with this throw you must attack while they move. Quite often they will either be travelling away from you or in a circular direction, and it is important that you choose the correct time to attack. This comes when they have just taken a step and their legs are spaced apart. As you are able to see in the photographs 3a, b, c, balance plays a vital role in

this technique as Brian Jacks, one of Britain's greatest judoka, rotates on his right leg using his left leg to spin his body in the direction he wishes to throw. It is the force of his rotating body plus the final thrust from his legs that spins his opponent on to his back.

This particular throw was used by Brian in the final of the 1978 British Open Championships, a bout which lasted precisely eight seconds.

*3a, b, c  Brian Jacks rotates on his right leg, using his left leg to spin his body in the direction he wishes to throw*

## TAI-OTOSHI – BODY DROP THROW

Tai-otoshi is also one of the most popular forward throwing techniques and presently there are many variations being used in international judo.

With my own tai-otoshi I have two particular ways of gripping which have proved to be very successful in competition. One is a conventional grip and the other is a yama-arashi grip.

# Neil Adams

In photograph 4 you can see that my legs are at a slight diagonal compared to my opponent's so that my right leg and foot can go slightly behind my partner's to trap his right leg and prevent him from stepping over. Both my legs are slightly bent and it is the straightening of the legs, the pulling of the sleeve and the pushing with the lapel that rotates my opponent over.

> **TIP**
>
> My points of body contact can change all the time, depending on the type of tai-otoshi and the height of my opponent. Try to feel what points of contact work best for you and experiment with different sizes of judoka.

4 Demonstrating tai-otoshi

# Karen Briggs

Karen Briggs performs a very low tai-otoshi which is completed at immense speed. As you can see in photographs 4a, b, c, on page 27, her points of body contact are very low, and without needing a very strong hand-pulling action she rotates her opponent on to their back for a successful score.

Quite often tai-otoshi is described as a hand throw, which I think is only partly right. The body plays just as important a role in this technique and I feel it would be a mistake to single this down to any one particular part of the body.

# David Starbrook

David Starbrook, Olympic silver medallist, is a tai-otoshi specialist and was without doubt one of the physically strongest judoka ever to step on to a mat. However, he was also one of the most unsupple.

It was impossible for David to split his legs very far at all. Therefore his body contact with his opponent was a lot higher when he attacked. His speed of entry for the throw was extremely fast, and what David failed to do with his legs, he made up for with hands and upper body. In fact he used perhaps 90% of his upper body for the technique. A powerful pulling action and body rotation were enough to rotate his opponents on to their backs.

In photograph 5, David's amazing pulling action compensates for his straight

5 David Starbrook demonstrating his very strong tai-otoshi

legs. Imagine if he had been flexible as well!

# Neil Adams

My last example of tai-otoshi is one with a variation of the grip although the actual movement in the technique is similar to the normal tai-otoshi.

The yama-arashi grip uses both hands to hold on to one side of the jacket, one on the lapel and the other on the sleeve, as demonstrated in photograph 6a. As you can see, I have only gripped my opponent's lapel and I wait for him to move his arm towards me before gripping the sleeve and attacking simultaneously (remember; it is forbidden to grip both sides of the jacket without attacking

6a Tai-otoshi using the yama-arashi grip . . .

*b, c . . .notice the control with both hands*

immediately). In photographs 6b, c, you can see the strong pulling action I can get with this grip. Still maintaining my leg contact, I prevent my opponent from stepping over my leg.

> **TIP**
>
> The yama-arashi grip is well worth mastering because it is awkward to fight against and can be advantageous when fighting a very one-sided judoka whose techniques would prevent normal gripping.

# TOMOE-NAGE – STOMACH THROW

As with all the other techniques there are a number of tomoe-nage variations and it is one of the most popular 'sacrifice' techniques used in modern-day judo. Although most popular with the lighter-weight categories it is sometimes used by the heavier weights and with considerable success.

Yoko-tomoe-nage (side stomach throw) is the most widely used variation because it can be operated from a distance requiring only initial foot contact and a specialized hand movement to finish. The body positioning is the key factor in determining direction with yoko-tomoe-nage and can also decide which leg the person attacks with.

The beauty of tomoe-nage and yoko-tomoe-nage is that either leg can be used, and many directions are possible.

# Karen Briggs – right leg

In photograph 7a Karen Briggs' right attacking leg is some distance from her partner and the distance between them is very important in order that an almost straight right leg can be placed into her opponent's stomach. This enables her body to swing towards the left leg of her opponent, see 7b. Now that their balance has been lost, Karen's left leg prevents her opponent from stepping forward and simultaneously sweeps the right leg away. With the two legs operating a scissor-type movement (7c) and the strong pulling action with the hands controlling her opponent's arm, she is able to throw for an ippon.

In photograph 7d Karen throws her opponent with a variation of yoko-tomoe-nage. Note her strong pulling action and the control she has with the attacking leg.

*7a, b, c, d Karen Briggs using her right leg and strong pulling action for tomoe-nage*

# Ingrid Berghmans – left leg

As I mentioned earlier, it is possible for tall judoka to throw successfully with yoko-tomoe-nage and this sequence shows Ingrid Berghmans throwing with another variation. Instead of using her right leg, she uses her left. Photographs 8a, b, show how Ingrid has created a space between herself and her opponent in which to move. This is achieved with a strong pulling action on the opponent's sleeve. She then places her left foot at about the same level as their belt and bends her leg in order to drop underneath them. In 8c, d, Ingrid has pulled strongly on the opponent's sleeve and straightened her leg in order to direct and throw them. As you can see in 8e the strength used by Ingrid to throw the opponent has forced them to travel a considerable distance. For this technique Ingrid would be moving towards her left side and her leg would then determine her opponent's exact landing place.

> **TIP**
>
> Although this technique can be done statically, you will find it more effective if you and your opponent are on the move, which is also easier for tall judoka.

*8a, b, c, d, e Ingrid Berghmans using her left leg for tomoe-nage*

# Katsuhiko Kashiwazaki

Photographs 9a, b, c, d, illustrate one of the finest examples of yoko-tomoe-nage as performed by Katsuhiko Kashiwazaki of Japan (World Champion 1981, five times all-Japan weight category champion – U 65 kg). It is always done on the move and to start the technique he uses an extremely strong kuzushi (breaking of balance). This is achieved with a strong pulling action on the sleeve in order to bend his opponent over. It gets an automatic reaction, with his opponent trying to straighten up. The space is now created for the movement and Kashiwazaki spins underneath, placing his left foot into his opponent's stomach. With fantastic agility he almost does a backward somersault to maintain control of his opponent so that he can make a follow-up attack in ne-waza.

One of the biggest problems judoka have when attacking with yoko-tomoe-nage is deciding which foot to use for each direction. It really does not matter as long as you are able to control the movement and direct your opponent on to their back.

*9a, b, c, d  Katsuhiko Kashiwazaki's famous yoko-tomoe-nage*

# Kerrith Brown – double-footed

In photograph 10 we see the double-footed yoko-tomoe-nage. It is a speciality of Kerrith Brown of Great Britain, six times British Open Champion, Olympic bronze medallist in the 1984 Los Angeles Olympics, European silver medallist in 1986 and World bronze medallist in 1987.

He attacks so quickly for the technique that his opponent becomes confused and wonders which direction he will land in. Because of his opponent's confusion he brings in his second foot to be used as a stabilizer in order to direct the throw.

This double-footed yoko-tomoe-nage has won Kerrith many important competitions.

*10  The double-footed yoko-tomoe-nage – a speciality of Kerrith Brown*

## O-UCHI-GARI – MAJOR INNER REAPING, AND
## KO-UCHI-GARI – MINOR INNER REAPING

These are both rear throws and can be extremely dynamic when linked with a forward attack. Often when an opponent is strongly resisting a forward attack they become momentarily vulnerable to a rear attack. This, of course, can also work the other way round, and o-uchi-gari and ko-uchi-gari are often used for combination techniques, although they should always be considered as individual throws.

The first examples of each show the same basic principles, but attacking the opponent's opposite sides. In both cases the legs and hands are very important to the technique and although total body contact is not necessary, its use can be vital.

In both o-uchi-gari and ko-uchi-gari the technique must be coordinated as the opponent steps forward.

# Neil Adams – o-uchi-gari

As you can see in the first variation of o-uchi-gari, I attack my opponent as he advances with his left leg. At this point my hand movement is important in pulling my partner's weight on to his left leg. I use my right lapel grip which pulls his shoulder downwards so that all his weight is on his supporting left leg. I then use my right leg to firstly hook and then sweep his leg away – 11.

The danger of being counterattacked becomes greater the more side-on your body is when commencing the attack. To complete the attack the hips should rotate until they are parallel to your opponent's, then finish between their legs when they land on their back.

11 Demonstrating o-uchi-gari

# Neil Adams – ko-uchi-gari

Again this attack is initiated as the opponent advances forward, only this time with the right leg. Photograph 12a shows the importance of my sleeve and lapel grips in pulling my opponent's weight over the foot that I sweep away. Notice the driving action in 12b as I sweep his supporting leg away.

The use of the head helps determine the direction in which my opponent falls – you can see that I am looking at the spot where I want to throw him.

> **TIP**
>
> Experiment with using your head in different techniques and remember that it can be used just as effectively for both forward and backward techniques.

*12a, b This shows the importance of my sleeve and lapel grips in pulling my opponent's weight over the foot that I sweep away*

# Ingrid Berghmans – o-uchi-gari

In photograph 13a Ingrid Berghmans begins her o-uchi-gari from a distance and moves in closer to obtain the body contact she requires with her opponent for the technique, see 13b. Her high lapel grip around the back of her opponent's head pulls him downwards to place all his body weight on his supporting leg. She then sweeps this leg away and finishes between his legs – photographs 13c, d.

*13a, b, c, d Ingrid begins her o-uchi-gari from a distance, then moves in closer, and sweeps away her opponent's supporting leg*

# Neil Adams – ko-uchi-gari (hand assisted)

This variation is operated from a distance with the coordination of hands and legs. The advantage of this type of ko-uchi-gari is that you don't necessarily need to use both hands to grip your opponent.

In photograph 14 I have secured a lapel grip. I then stretch my leg out and scoop my opponent's right foot towards me. Before he can put his foot down again I catch his leg with my left hand and drive forward to finish the technique by pushing with my lapel grip against my opponent's upper body.

*14 Ko-uchi-gari (hand assisted)*

## OSOTO-GARI – MAJOR OUTER REAPING

Osoto-gari is a very dynamic backward throw with many variations for entry into it. The technique also involves two important leg actions, which are hooking and sweeping.

# Hooking

This technique is very often performed with the two judoka starting some distance away from one another and with the attacker hooking the opponent's furthermost leg. In order to do this the attacker stretches their right leg out and hooks the opponent's rear leg. At this point the attacker has not moved their left leg. Once

the right leg has made contact the opponent braces in defence for the throw. The attacker now hops their left leg into position to sweep the opponent's legs away. The hands are used to pull the opponent's weight on to the leg being hooked and finish the technique by pulling the lapel grip upwards and pushing the sleeve grip downwards.

> **TIP**
>
> The hopping action of your left leg should be done at speed so that there is no danger of being counterattacked with the same technique. This is because as you hop there is momentarily no contact with the floor, and a slow hop could leave you vulnerable to a counterattack.

15  Hooking – osoto-gari

# Sweeping

Ingrid Berghmans demonstrates this technique. She has a great advantage with this variation because of the control she has of her opponent's head. In photograph 16a Ingrid has pulled her opponent's body over so that all his weight is on his right leg. Her dominant collar grip around the opponent's neck means that she can push her arm against his head to force it backwards, which helps break her opponent's balance. As Ingrid does this she steps forward on to her left leg so that she is on the same parallel as her opponent. Photo-

16a, b, c, d Ingrid demonstrates a sweeping osoto-gari

graph 16b shows her swinging her sweeping foot forwards and then backwards in order to sweep away her opponent's right leg.

In photograph 16c the contact point, from the knee joint to the foot, between both judoka's legs is illustrated. Ingrid's strong pulling action with the sleeve grip rotates her opponent on to their back to finish the throw, as seen in photograph 16d.

# THE UNORTHODOX TECHNIQUES

Although Western judo already had a range of 'pick-up' techniques, other techniques such as ura-nage (rear throw), kata-garuma (shoulder wheel) and te-garuma (hand throw) were developed by the Russians in the early 1960s as variations.

Western judo soon began to take a special interest in these techniques when the Russians used them to take advantage of every competitive judo situation and skilfully turn someone's mistake to their advantage.

# Ura-nage

These dynamic ura-nage attacks by Chochoshvilli of the Soviet Union show his 100% commitment to the technique with his body completely arched backwards.

## Variation 1

Chochoshvilli's fantastic leg movement firstly lifts his opponent and then drives him backwards towards the mat – see photographs 17a, b, c.

> **TIP**
>
> Practise this technique with the aid of a crash mat so that you can get the full commitment required for an effective throw.

*17a, b, c Chochoshvilli's fantastic leg movement lifts his opponent and drives him backwards towards the mat*

# Variation 2

The difference with this ura-nage attack by Chochoshvilli is that unlike the first variation, where he takes advantage of his opponent's poor attack, this time he is the one to initiate the movement. As you can see in photographs 18a, b, c, his opponent is facing him. Chochoshvilli once again elevates his opponent with a strong lifting action using his left leg. This is coordinated with a strong pulling action with the hands to turn his opponent on to their back. In this particular attack Chochoshvilli gave his full commitment to the technique, so much so that his own head hit the mat first and rendered him almost unconscious. Amazingly, he was given a waza-ari (seven small points) for the throw but lost the match to Uemura of Japan (1975 World Champion, 1976 Olympic Champion) who held him down for an ippon, probably because he was too dazed to defend.

*18a, b, c This time
Chochoshvilli initiates the
attack facing his opponent*

# Kata-garuma

Kata-garuma requires a powerful lifting action with the legs and is executed very quickly. With an orthodox sleeve grip and the other hand free to place between the opponent's legs, the attacker must get underneath the opponent in order to lift them up.

As with all other lifting actions, the back should be straight and the legs alone should do the lifting work. Once the opponent is on your shoulders the direction in which you choose to throw them depends on what movements they make to try to escape the throw.

## Variation 1 – side/forwards

In photograph 19, Bodavelli of the USSR has an extremely strong kata-garuma attack and initiates the technique with a pulling action from the hand he places between his opponent's legs, clamping hold firmly of one leg and pulling them towards him. He then bends his legs in order to get underneath his opponent and places his head in their armpit. A strong pull on the sleeve grip and a push with the other hand projects his opponent over on to their back. This is done in either a forward or sidewards direction.

*19  Bodavelli of the Soviet
Union disposes of his opponent*

## Variation 2 – backwards

This technique looks very similar to the first variation. The attacker has the opponent on his or her shoulders. The difference is that to finish the technique the attacker arches their back and throws the opponent to the rear rather than to the front. This technique can be dangerous and should only be practised with the aid of a crash mat: 20a, b, c.

*20a, b, c  This fine example shows Takeshi Mizushima throwing his opponent to his rear rather than to the front*

# Morote-gari – double hand throw

Although morote-gari shows certain similarities to a rugby tackle, it is in fact a very skilful movement that requires good coordination and a quick entry – see photograph 21. This technique rarely scores an ippon, but often produces a useful small score.

The secret of the entry into the throw is to make your opponent think that they are taking a normal upper body grip. This ensures that they are in an upright position and not jigotai (defensive). Then, very quickly you duck underneath your opponent's arms and scoop their legs from underneath them with both your hands. You are then able to finish the technique either by focusing them backwards or to the side depending on their resistance to the technique.

I think this technique seldom scores the maximum ippon because there is no upper body control. However, it almost always gets a score.

I'm finishing this chapter with some of the effective but unorthodox techniques because fighters are always looking for new techniques and variations of the old ones. You can do the same in your everyday practise by looking at the techniques with an open mind and forming your own particular variations of them.

> **TIP**
>
> Practise all tachi-waza techniques with different types of grips. This will give you many options for attack and increase your range of techniques.

*21  Robert van der Walle specializes in morote-gari*

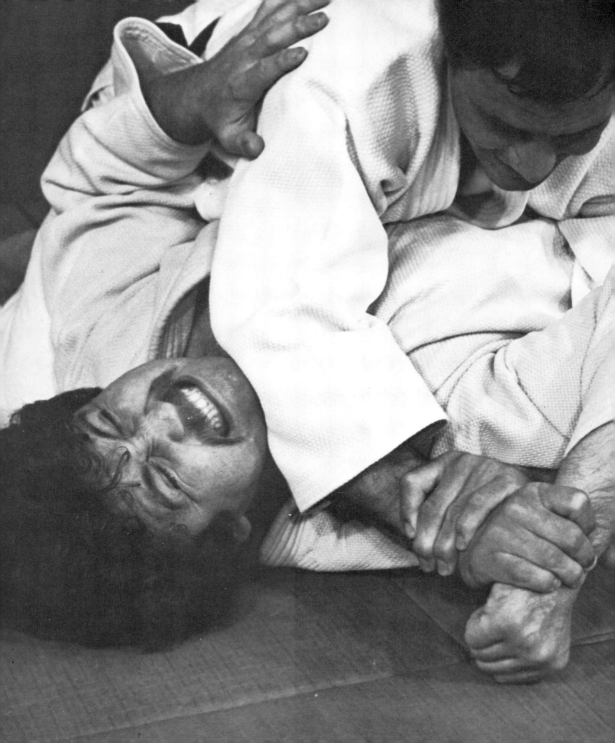

# Ne-waza – groundwork

There are so many techniques in ne-waza that in this chapter, as with the tachi-waza chapter, I have chosen the most popular ones used in practice and competition.

The main aim in ne-waza is to immobilize your opponent by either holding them on their back for a thirty-second period, armlocking, or strangling them for a submission.

For children under the age of sixteen, the practise of kansetsu-waza and shime-waza is not permitted because they can be dangerous if applied quickly, and so it is important that care is taken whilst practising them.

Many people favour ne-waza to tachi-waza because of the vast number of variations to be learned. In tachi-waza a good judoka will usually only master three or four techniques, whereas a good ne-waza specialist will probably master many more. Unlike tachi-waza, where the Gokyo consists of forty throwing techniques, a ne-waza Gokyo has never been formulated. It was thought in the early days that ne-waza was not as important as tachi-waza, althought I believe it is equally as important. A ne-waza Gokyo would be an interesting prospect, although there are so many variations of techniques that it would be difficult to know what should be omitted.

Good ne-waza skills compliment tachi-waza by giving complete confidence for a fully commited tachi-waza attack. It means that your judo skills will be better balanced.

In judo competitions you are only allowed a split second to follow from tachi-waza into ne-waza, therefore it is important to practise as much as possible linking both forms of technique together.

## OSAE-KOMI-WAZA – HOLDING TECHNIQUES

These are some of the more popular holding techniques with one or two variations on each.

To score an ippon with osae-komi-waza you must hold your opponent for thirty seconds; for a waza-ari, twenty-five seconds; for a yuko, twenty seconds; and for a koka, ten seconds.

> **TIP**
> All holdings require body and head control.

# Hon-kesa-gatame – basic scarf hold

This technique is one of the first osae-komi-waza taught to most beginners. It is very popular because it is easy to go from a throwing technique into this hold.

## Variation 1 – Ingrid Berghmans

Ingrid Berghmans is demonstrating in photograph 1 her own particular hon-kesa-gatame. She often uses this in international competition, which shows it is by no means used only by beginners.

The term 'scarf hold' is used because tori's arm is placed around uke's neck securing the head. Her left arm is pulling her partner's right arm across her chest. As you can see, Ingrid is lying by the side of her partner and has body contact to pin her opponent to the mat. By spreading her legs she can use them to stabilize herself

1

and compensate for her partner's attempts to escape from the technique.

## Variation 2

The hold automatically changes into kuzure-kesa-gatame (kuzure means broken, or variation) if tori in any way changes arm control This often happens when uke bridges in order to escape and tori moves the arm from around the neck and uses it once again to stabilize themself – see photograph 2.

Whilst using this technique many judoka have their heads next to their opponents' heads. Referring back to photograph 1, Ingrid's head is above her partner's chest because of the strong pulling action of her hands, which she uses to put extra pressure on her opponent's body.

2

# Hon-kami-shiho-gatame – upper four quarters

## Variation 1

For the basic hon-kami-shiho-gatame, lie face down on your partner with your head facing their feet. Pass both hands under uke's shoulders and grip their belt with both hands at the side of their waist, as in photograph 3.

Uke's head should be controlled by tori, trapping it with their elbow and pulling it against the trunk of their body. The legs once again play a very important part in the adjustment of tori's balance in order to compensate for uke's movements.

3

## Variation 2

Sometimes the knees are brought up so that tori is in a crouched position. Tori can then use their legs to adjust their body so that the necessary body contact is made. Constant body contact is kept when tori lies flat and pushes their hips into the mat, see photograph 4.

4

## Broken variation – kuzure-kami-shiho-gatame

5

This is a technique in which tori varies their hand control by taking either or both of their hands over the top of uke's arms, sometimes gripping the belt and sometimes with the arm around uke's shoulder gripping the collar behind the neck, as in photograph 5. This can ensure complete immobilization of uke's upper body.

# Hon-yoko-shiho-gatame – side four quarters

Hon-yoko-shiho-gatame is used frequently by top judoka because different techniques are easy to move into from the side-four-quarters position.

## Variation 1

Once again, lie face down on top of uke, but this time at a right angle to them. The knees can be brought up into a crouching position (photograph 6) in order to counter your partner's movements.

6

## Variation 2

If you are trying to hold down someone very strong it is better to flatten your body in order to prevent the possibility of their lifting you off, as, for example, in photograph 7.

To secure both forms of hon-yoko-shiho-gatame, tori should press their head and chest to uke's chest, passing one hand under and behind uke's neck to grip their lapel with their thumb inside. The other hand should be placed between uke's legs and grip uke's belt at the side. If your opponent is taller than you, it is sometimes difficult to reach the belt and at the same time have control of uke's upper body. At all times control the head and chest and, if necessary, grip uke's trouser leg instead of the belt.

7

## Kuzure-yoko-shiho-gatame (broken variation)

You cannot always control the whole of uke's body, so slight variations with both hands by tori are sometimes necessary. I have already mentioned the holding of the trouser leg and for this it is best to control the leg at the knee joint. The other hand can also change from being around the neck, and there are a number of other variations that you can try. In photograph 8 tori has placed their right arm over uke's chest in order to keep the head and shoulders under control. This variation can be used to stop uke from escaping by sitting up.

*8*

# *Tate-shiho-gatame – vertical four quarters*

One of the most effective osae-komi-waza today is tate-shiho-gatame, with numerous turnovers from the many situations leading into this technique. Karen Briggs is particularly skilful and often links her tomoe-nage with tate-shiho-gatame. For this technique it is important that control of the opponent's head is kept at all times and that your legs are used to immobilize the lower half of your opponent's body. This can be achieved by pushing your mid-section into your opponent and crossing your feet underneath them to make it impossible for them to escape.

## SHIME-WAZA – STRANGLE TECHNIQUES

There are two basic methods of strangulation. The first is the choke, which is pressure applied against the front of uke's throat, thus preventing uke from breathing. The second is the strangle in the true sense which requires pressure at each side of the neck, cutting off the blood supply to the brain. Both can be very effective, **but should be practised with caution.**

# Hadaka-jime – naked strangle

My first example is hadaka-jime, which is a choke technique. It translates as 'naked strangle' because the use of neither uke's nor tori's jacket is required and only the hands and arms are used for its application.

In photograph 9 you can see tori's left hand and forearm against uke's throat. Both tori's hands are then clasped together and uke is pulled backwards with tori pushing uke's head forwards with their shoulder. The pulling action by tori, whilst pushing uke's head forwards, applies the hadaka-jime, forcing a quick submission.

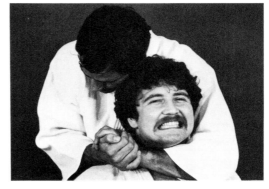

9

# Kata-juji-jime – fingers and thumb/ Nami-juji-jime – both thumbs/ Gyaku-juji-jime – fingers only

I have demonstrated all these shime-waza together because they are very similar, and I think many judoka get them mixed up.

## Kata-juji-jime

In photograph 10 uke is facing tori before applying the kata-juji-jime. Tori's right hand slides across uke's chest and grips uke's right lapel as high round the collar as possible with the fingers inside. Tori then passes their left hand across their own forearm and places their thumb inside the collar – again, as high round the neck as possible. The kata-juji-jime is then applied

10

by pulling down with the hands, applying pressure to the side of the neck, and outwards with the elbows.

## Nami-juji-jime

In photograph 11 you can see that nami-juji-jime is very similar to kata-juji-jime. Tori's right hand slides across uke's chest, this time placing their thumb on the inside of uke's collar. Tori then passes their left hand over their own forearm and places the other thumb inside the left collar. The nami-juji-jime is then applied in the same manner, by pulling downwards with the hands and outwards with the elbows.

11

## Gyaku-juji-jime

12

This variation is applied in the same way as the other two. Photograph 12 shows that this time tori's fingers are both placed inside uke's left and right lapels.

When attempting any of these shime-waza techniques, it is essential that you have full control of your opponent with your legs. Often they can be applied whilst tori is on their back and uke is between tori's legs. Once tori has complete control of uke the shime-waza can then be executed.

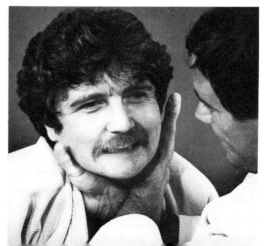

# Sangaku-jime – triangular strangle

Sangaku-jime is a strangle which is applied with the legs. It is called a triangular strangle because both of tori's legs form a triangular shape around uke's head and arm.

## Variation 1

In photograph 13a you can see that tori is lying on their back and uke is again between tori's legs. Tori, who would have started facing uke, has turned their body at right angles to uke in order that the right knee joint will go around the back of uke's neck. Tori then puts their right foot behind their own left knee joint making sure that they control uke's right arm, see photograph 13b. For the application of this shime-waza you must have uke's arm within the triangle. This is because pressure on uke's neck only is not allowed. Now simply squeeze with both legs in order to obtain a submission. If the shime-waza is not quite 'on', try adjusting your hips slightly to gain a better contact and pull your opponent's arm towards you.

13a

13b

## Variation 2

Another very easy way to learn sangaku-jime is with both judoka lying on their backs with you partner (uke) resting their head on your leg. Now take your right leg round your partner's right arm and head and secure the triangular leg position by putting your left foot behind your right knee. This is so much easier to do when

*14a, b Notice my right foot is behind my left knee in order to control my opponent's head and arms*

simultaneously turning your hips towards your partner's head in order to get the correct adjustment with the legs. The shime-waza is made more effective if your opponent's free arm is pulled towards you and you have their other arm at all times under control by securing it with their own belt or judo-gi. This is illustrated in photographs 14a and b.

## KANSETSU-WAZA – ARMLOCKS: JOINT TECHNIQUES

There are two particular ways of applying armlocks and both are against the elbow joints. This is because wrist locks and shoulder locks are not always easy to control and so could became dangerous if applied during competition. Pressure can be applied against the elbow joint, either when the arm is straight or when the arm is bent, and should be released immediately once a submission has been made.

# *Ude-gatame – straight armlock*

The first variation of a straight armlock is one that can also be used in tachi-waza as well as ne-waza, as long as an immediate submission is obtained. This technique is often used when uke has gripped either of tori's lapels. Tori then uses their hands to take a firm grip of uke's elbow and controls uke's lapel grip by pressing their head downwards against the hand and wrist. The lock is then applied by tori moving their body backwards or to the side so that they are able to pull against the elbow and gain a submission.

# Juji-gatame – straight armlock

Juji-gatame is one of the most frequently used of all the armlocks and there are now many different ways of applying it from lots of positions. In photograph 15 my opponent is on his back and both my legs are being used to control him. My right leg is under my partner's chin and controls his head and shoulders, preventing him from sitting up. My left leg is across the chest and should be used to control the midsection. Contact between my underside and my partner's underside is important in order to keep constant control of the arm which is between my legs.

*15 Juji-gatame is one of the most popular of all armlocks*

To apply the lock I have gripped my opponent's wrist with both hands and extend the arm across my middle. I now lift my hips upwards to apply pressure to the elbow joint.

> **TIP**
> Remember that the legs play a very big part in juji-gatame and should always be controlling uke.

# Ude-garami – bent armlock

Often when uke feels in danger of being armlocked with a straight armlock they will resist by bending their arm to relieve the pressure. This leaves many opportunities for ude-garami. Here is one example: in photograph 16, tori lies across uke's chest, gripping the wrist with the left hand. They then put their right arm under uke's upper

16

left arm and catch hold of their own wrist. In photograph 17, the ude-garami is then applied by pushing the wrist downwards and driving the elbow upwards with your right arm. A slight twisting movement at the same time can make the ude-garami more effective. Ude-garami can also be done from beneath.

17

## TURNOVERS

It's all very well knowing how to perform certain techniques and how to apply them, but the biggest problem is to be able to manoeuvre an opponent into these moves.

There are of course many different turnovers, so I have chosen just the most popular ones.

# Turnover – off knees

I have covered this situation throughout the book because it is one of the most common attacking positions for all techniques in ne-waza. To begin the technique you need to have control of uke's two lapels. To reach these simply put your hands underneath both of uke's armpits and secure a firm grip on each lapel. Now roll on to your back making sure that full control of your partner is kept at all times. You are now in the attacking position and have a choice between: osae-komi-waza, kansetsu-waza or shime-waza.

# Sangaku – turnover

In photograph 18 Ingrid Berghmans has full control of uke's head by pulling it downwards into the mat, preventing them from standing up. She then hooks uke's left arm in order to use it to lever them on to their back. Her left leg would then slide in between uke's right arm and leg and she would fall on to her left shoulder, turning her partner on to their back. She now has a choice of techniques that she can use and must maintain control with her legs at all times.

18

# Juji-gatame-sangaku-jime – roll

Photograph 19a shows one of the most popular starting positions for juji-gatame, with tori attacking uke when they are on their knees. Normally tori's right leg would pass underneath uke's head in order to turn them over for the juji-gatame, but in this case uke has defended by gripping tori's leg. This now means that tori must change the technique although they will still have to apply pressure to uke's head in order to turn them on to their back. Tori's left hand should at all times maintain control of uke's left hand simply by gripping the wrist. Now tori pushes their right leg against the side of uke's head and tries to direct their face upwards towards the ceiling with their leg, as in photograph 19b. This makes him

Above right: *19a* Right: *19b*

Clockwise: *19c, d, e, f, g*

turn on to his back in order to relieve the pressure. Now tori pushes uke's head forward to prevent them from turning away from tori and at the same time turns sideways so that their right leg folds neatly around uke's neck, see photographs 19c and 19d. Photographs 19e and 19f are close-ups of the sangaku-jime with photograph 19e showing the right foot behind the left knee. In photograph 19f the left foot is then placed underneath uke's underside and the strangle continues. If tori then turns their hips upwards so that they are underneath uke's head, they can straighten out uke's arm by applying a double sangaku-juji-gatame technique.

---

**TIP**

As with tachi-waza, the variations of all these techniques are forever increasing. Study them and try to work out some of your own variations. You really will never stop learning new ones!

---

# Tactical play

As in all sports, judo has its own forms of tactical play. Although the rules are there to be adhered to, it is the ability of the judoka to use these rules to their advantage that can make the vital difference between winning and losing.

There are many judoka who always seem to win competitions even though they do not possess formidable attacks in either tachi-waza or ne-waza. This they manage to do mostly through their use of the rules. After all, they are there to be used and can even be bent a little.

For me, though, the supreme judoka has good physical condition, excellent tachi-waza and ne-waza, and the ability to play tactical judo if need be.

## PLAYING THE MAT AREA

There is a one-metre-wide red area surrounding the contest area, and this we class as the 'danger area'. Once you are in the red zone you know that there is a possibility of penalization if you have stepped outside the contest area purposely.

This means that by manoeuvring an opponent towards this area, you have immediately put them on the alert, making them cautious. Thinking of an escape from the 'danger area' can be dangerous for them. It means they have only two alternative escape routes, either to your left or right side. Once they have chosen either one or the other, you then have an opportunity for attacking. If your opponent is panicked into attacking you at the edge of the contest area, and part of their body touches the outside of the contest area before yours does, this can be classed as an infringement of the rules and they can be penalized.

Playing within the danger area can be a very hazardous game, especially if the stakes are high and if the referee has perhaps not read the contest quite as you have been playing it. If, for example, the contestant at the edge of the contest area is pushed out deliberately, then the fighter doing the pushing is penalized. It is, however, very difficult to push someone outside the contest area if they resist.

Therefore, if you were to step ouside it could, depending on the referee's discretion, result in you being penalized.

Many penalties given in the danger area are won by clever tactical play, and one twitch with the legs or hands can make an opponent at the edge overreact to what they think is going to be an attack, thus making them step out of the area. It's not really judo, but certainly within the rules and many times it can be the deciding score in a contest.

# NE-WAZA EDGE PLAY

There was a time when anyone who did not want to participate in ne-waza would immediately make a dash to the outside of the contest area in order to break the contest. The contest would then be resumed in their favourite tachi-waza position. Nowadays this is not allowed, and anyone who leaves the mat edge deliberately in ne-waza or tachi-waza is immediately penalized. If you should, however, roll out of the area while avoiding an attack, the contest would be stopped and then resumed again in the middle of the mat. One of the most effective ways to break the contest when in danger, i.e. when someone is on your back, is to look for the edge and deliberately roll with your opponent outside the contest area. The problem for the referee is to decide whether or not it was a deliberate act! This decision is with the referees. Sometimes you may get away with it and other times you will not. Many clever tactical fighters can, however, disguise such an action. After all, in the 'heat' of a contest it is very difficult to know exactly where the edge of the area is, and if you go outside accidentally there is no penalty.

You can also turn the edge play to your advantage when your partner is too close to the edge, especially when you suspect that your opponent does not want to continue to fight in ne-waza. This can result in a panic situation with your opponent doing anything possible to break the contest so that it will be resumed in tachi-waza. It is possible to encourage the referee's disapproval of this action by making it obvious that you were trying to keep your opponent not only in ne-waza but in the centre of the mat. If they should pull away too vigorously or pull away and step outside the contest area, they can once again be penalized.

Tactical play at the edge of the contest area should only be attempted by experienced judoka, although I have seen world-class competitors misjudge a situation and get heavily penalized for it. Be careful!

# GRIPPING (THE JUDO-GI)

Modern-day judo is dominated by specialized gripping tactics, and it is becoming more and more difficult to attain personalized special grips in order to make positive attacks. Gone are the days of the big judo-gi that looked like a bell tent and was easy to grip, although larger kimonos are being reintroduced. In the mid-1970s tailored judo-gi were first introduced – there was a minimum requirement for the size of the judo-gi, and as long as it was not made any smaller it was not against the rules. This immediately gave a different meaning to the gripping tactics and to tactical play in general. After all, if you are unable to throw your opponent you have to try and win another way.

2 *The traditional grip*

3 *The variation grip*

The thickness of the material also has a maximum and a minimum requirement. The texture of the material can also make a big difference when you are gripping. Many top fighters take the judo-gi measurements to the absolute minimum size required, but with new requirements being introduced advocating larger sleeves and generally more material to be worn, I hope that the emphasis on gripping will perhaps change a little so that more attacking can be done and less gripping tactics played. The small judo-gi is not everyone's choice, however, and sometimes fighters find it too restrictive, almost like fighting in a straight-jacket. Brian Jacks, for example, always used to wear loose judo-gi because he felt that he had more space to move and did not feel so restricted. They were also ideal for conveniently slipping out of when someone attacked him, and many times I have seen him in competition with a very bewildered opponent having thrown Brian's jacket for a full ippon. Unfortunately, though, Brian was never in it at the time.

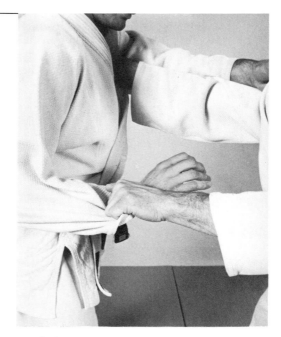

4  *The low sleeve grip*

# GRIPPING TACTICS

As I said earlier, sometimes a whole contest can go by without a proper or meaningful attack being made by either fighter. This may be because one or the other is concentrating so hard on not letting a proper grip be taken on their jacket that they do not really have enough time to make a full attack themself. However, they may also be preventing an opponent from attacking as well. The result of such gripping tactics can be a very negative contest. Try and use these tactics in order to perform positive judo.

5 *The yama-arashi two-sided grip*

# The sleeves

A bent arm is much more difficult to grip than a straight one, especially if you point your elbow towards your partner. This pulls the material of the sleeve much tighter and leaves the elbow joint and the material surrounding it very taut and virtually impossible to hold. If your opponent does manage to grip your sleeve, the same procedure can be followed to break the grip. Bend your arm with your elbow towards your opponent and snatch away your arm quickly and firmly. Be careful when practising this as it can be very painful indeed when it happens to you!

Sometimes, when your opponent has a firm grip on your sleeve and the first tactic does not work, you can counteract their strong grip by crossing your hand over to their opposite lapel. This not only makes it very awkward for your opponent to attack because your fist is against their shoulder, but also gives you an opportunity for a yama-arashi attacking movement. Another method of breaking their sleeve grip is to put your hand behind your own knee and use the power from both your leg and hand to pull backwards in order to break the grip.

Do not spend a whole contest trying to get your favourite sleeve grip. Look for other opportunities as well and do not forget that a double lapel grip can be very effective if used in the correct way.

*6a, b, c One way of breaking your opponent's lapel grip is to catch their sleeve and apply pressure against the elbow joint. They may at least release their grip, and even submit to an armlock*

87

# The lapel grip

A simple gripping tactic to prevent your opponent from gripping your lapels is simply to hold your own lapel and slide your hand upwards or downwards depending on which part your opponent is trying to grip. This can be done with either hand and means that your opponent grips your hand instead of the jacket. If they have gripped your lapel and you wish to break the grip, take hold of the lapel near to your partner's hand and pull the lapel taut. Now pull back sharply and you will find that your opponent will find it very difficult to maintain their grip. With new rules for the sizes of judo-gi being introduced all the time, the tactics will obviously change as well. One thing is certain: if you can throw from a variation of grips, your opponents will find it increasingly difficult to stop you tactically. This then means that a whole different contest can take place.

*Opposite: 8 Notice how Ingrid totally dominates her opponent's shoulder with her high lapel grip*

*7a, b Ingrid has taken her opponent's lapel with her left hand in order to swing her right arm over to secure her favourite grip*

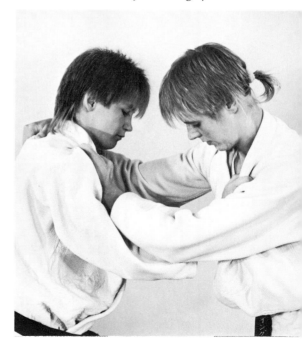

# TIME-WASTING

In the days when as much injury time as you wanted was allowed in a contest, masters of the fake injury would sometimes double the length of the contest by tactical time-wasting. Usually it was players in bad physical condition, or those who were under particular pressure who would stop the contest, beckon the doctor and spend the next two minutes bandaging a leg or an arm that was probably not injured. If this happened two or three times in the same contest it would break up the rhythm of the contest and could change the result. In competition now, injury time is not allowed and a doctor can only be beckoned to the mat once. If it is impossible for you to carry on with the contest it is automatically given to your opponent. It is amazing how quickly people recover now, and it is good that the contests run more smoothly.

There are still ways of wasting time, though, and one of the most popular is with what I call 'hit-and-run' tactics. The passivity ruling in judo is that you must make a positive attack at least every twenty seconds of the contest. The problem for the referee is to differentiate between a good attack and a time-wasting attack. If you are fighting someone who you know to be stronger than yourself, and you also feel in particular danger from their attacks, you can employ hit-and-run tactics. It is important that you judge when your opponent is going to attack you and make sure that you attack first, and that even if you do not think you will throw your opponent, you attack with as much force as possible. In between, you make sure that you are avoiding danger and that you look busy.

One of my best ever tactical contests was against Harald Heinke of East Germany in the final of the 1980 European Championships in the U78 kg category. I had been changing from the U71 kg category to the higher weight of U78 kg for one or two events because I realized that my eventual weight would be in the higher category. On this particular day I was approximately 74–75 kg and Heinke was coming down a weight from 84 kg to the U78 kg division. After the weigh-in you can eat quite normally and by the evening of the event Heinke looked every bit an 80 kg-plus fighter. He absolutely dwarfed me. It was a very tactical fight, and I was employing my hit-and-run tactics because at the time I felt like David fighting Goliath. I also knew that he did not like ne-waza, and at every possible opportunity I leapt on his back for my juji-gatame attack. I wasted almost a whole minute with each ne-waza attack and as the bell was signalled for the end of the contest I realized that I had won the title on attacks alone in both ne-waza and tachi-waza.

In the 1983 world final against Hikage of Japan I played a very similar tactical match against a very strong opponent, and thought that I had once again stolen the contest. This time, however, it went the other way, so if you play any kind of tactical game you are taking a chance on the final result.

# PSYCHOLOGY

Psychologically knowing you are the best can mean you are entering the contest with an advantage over your opponent. You can normally tell a confident competitor by the way he or she carries themself both before and during the contest. You might, however, be entering a contest and not necessarily be expected to win. It is here that personal psychology comes into play, and sometimes a little acting ability can pay dividends if it convinces your opponent that you are confident.

Often, competitors will stare at their opponents, or strut past them giving an arrogant smile that says 'I am going to beat you'. I have been intimidated many times by such actions, and have had to try to cover up my feelings and return the gesture. Deep down, though, both competitors are just as nervous as each other

and an arrogant display can sometimes indicate nervousness and lack of confidence. The difficulty is to show no emotion from such actions and not to let them effect your performance.

Muhammad Ali was the prime example of the loud, arrogant sportsman who outpsyched his opponents by making them angry and disturbing their concentration. Just as disturbing, though, are the competitors who show no feelings and no emotions. Such a competitor is Yasuhiro Yamashita, whose cool and collected composure gave people the impression that they were only fighting for second place and that they could not possibly spoil his day by beating him. Both are very different approaches and both very effective. Whatever you do, though, do not rely on them!

# CONCLUSION

It is very important to have a basic plan before entering into competition. This means doing a certain amount of study of the opposition. With the use of videos, the job has been made easier, although I believe that only limited information can

be drawn from them. I'm sure it is better, whenever possible, to watch your opponents at an event so that you can analyse their strengths and weaknesses. You might look out for the following.

# *Basic useful information*

(**A**) Are they right- or left-handed, or both?
(**B**) Do they favour tachi-waza or ne-waza, or both?
(**C**) Are they tactical fighters?
All these things are important to know so

that you can plan your lines of attack, most useful grips, and possible techniques that might score. It is important in judo *not* to have a fixed plan, and the biggest thing you should prepare for is the unexpected – which is one thing I should know!

1 *One of the most commonly used pulling actions*

# Uchi-komi training routines

Uchi-komi (utsu-komi) also means 'to beat against', 'to go in'. The importance of repetition or ingraining in any sport cannot be emphasized enough. If a technique is going to be performed spontaneously the movement must be practised over and over again. There can, however, be dangers with repetition practice, and it is easier to ingrain bad techniques instead of good techniques. This type of training should, therefore, always be monitored by a good coach.

Realistically, all techniques have to be performed within a movement, but it is important to break them down, master the fundamentals, and then put them all together again for a more realistic judo situation later.

The main problem for judoka wanting uchi-komi practise is that it is normally impossible to practise alone, so they need a good uke. Once a suitable partner has been found the technique-practice should be a team-effort learning process between uke and tori. A bad uke will be too tense and not allow their partner to mould into the techniques, getting the correct feeling for them.

To ingrain a technique successfully it must be broken down so that the judoka only has to think of one part of it at a time. By separating the three sections of hands, body and legs (as in the Fundamentals chapter page 25) and ensuring that each is mastered, you can then begin to practise the full repetition.

## TACHI-WAZA UCHI-KOMI

## Hands

Hand movements and grips vary with the technique practised. However, they always play an important role in the start and finish of any technique.

Kuzushi can be practised by pulling actions made with the hands. Taking a normal grip of uke, repeatedly pull them off balance. To achieve a good rhythm it is important that uke immediately resumes their original position between each repetition. Photograph 1 shows one of the most commonly used pulling actions for a tech-

93

nique and you should try to do sets of twenty repetitions. Your level of fitness will determine how many sets you are able to do. With this type of practice, the more you can do, the better.

The second important hand movement is one which breaks through your opponent's defending arms. This can be done with a normal grip holding the sleeve at the elbow and the inside lapel. By pulling your opponent towards you and simultaneously pulling their sleeve arm outwards and moving your inside lapel grip outwards, you are able to bend your opponent's stiff arms and therefore create enough space for an attack, see photograph 2. Once again, sets of twenty repetitions are recommended for this hand-movement practice.

I have covered the finishing hand movements later in this chapter because they can only be practised when completing the technique. See nage-komi (throwing practice) on page 100.

2 *Breaking through an opponent's defending arms*

# Body

There are numerous body movements that could be practised, but body contact and body turning are the main areas to cover. Body contact can be practised with the hand movements I have just mentioned, and finishing this time with full chest contact, as illustrated in photographs 3a and b. This type of body contact is most beneficial for rear throws, and once again you should do sets of twenty repetitions.

When practising forward-throwing uchi-komi, uke can play an important role in the correction of insufficient body contact. They can do this by constantly adjusting their body to help tori get the right contact.

Body-turning practice is used to help improve your speed of entry for an attack. It incorporates the use of the hips and the head to enable tori to spin his or her body into an attacking movement. It should be

*3a, b Here I get full chest contact by stepping towards my opponent, at the same time pulling him towards me and off balance*

stressed that this movement must be practised slowly at first, building up speed later to ensure that accuracy is not lost. This is one of the few occasions where it would be possible to practise without uke. This is called shadow uchi-komi, and works on the same principle as shadow boxing.

4

# *Legs*

Two main leg actions are required for most throwing techniques. They are the sweep and the hook and there are many variations of each.

## The sweep

I have given two examples of leg sweeping:

**Example 1** As you can see from photograph 4 I have over-emphasized my leg

5a

5b

action with the osoto-gari attack in order to practise the full sweeping movement. As you practise sweeping uchi-komi ask your partner to resist a little with their own leg. This will enable you to maintain a good rhythm and will make your exit from the technique easier, ready for you to start the next.

**Example 2**  For this I have used a forward

attacking movement and have once again over-emphasized the movement of my leg (photograph 5a) in order to sweep my partner off his feet (photograph 5b). For uchi-komi practice of this movement it is not necessary to throw your partner fully. However, it is better if you lift your partner a little off the ground to get a good feeling for the throw.

## The hook

For the practice of the osoto-gari hooking action in an uchi-komi movement a little resistance is required from uke. Uke should stand with the leg that you are going to attack a short distance from you.

Hook your partner's leg without moving your driving leg. In the photo sequence 6a, b, c, d, e, you can see that my driving leg is hooking my partner's leg at the knee joint. Repeat the movement twenty times, or more if you wish.

*7a, b I begin an o-uchi-gari attack with a hooking movement using my right leg, but my opponent resists, so I change direction and with a straight right leg sweep backwards for an uchi-mata*

## Combination: o-uchi-gari (hook); uchi-mata (sweep)

Hooking with the legs is another of my favourite movements. In photograph 7a I have started an o-uchi-gari attack with a hooking movement with my left leg. In photograph 7b my partner has resisted, so he changes direction and with a straight leg sweeps backwards for an uchi-mata attack. This can be practised in uchi-komi in one continuous movement. To keep a steady rhythm of attack it is not necessary to complete the throw every time. Start with a set of twenty uchi-komi and then increase the number of sets.

Once techniques have been broken down to their fundamental elements and these elements have been practised and mastered with uchi-komi, the fundamentals can be put together again to make a complete movement.

In the beginning it is better to start learning techniques in a static position so that all the elements of the technique work

*6a, b, c, d, e This hooking osoto-gari relies on a fast hooking action followed by strong upper body control to prevent a counterattack*

97

together correctly. I must point out, though, that techniques would very rarely be done from a static position and so the quicker you begin to practise them on the move, the better. However, it is important that you get used to operating all the elements of the throw together, and for that reason static uchi-komi has its purpose. Once you have laid the foundations for a technique it is important to start practising it in a more realistic manner with moving uchi-komi.

In a competitive situation there are an infinite number of directions your opponent might be moving in so a very relaxed randori practice with uke and tori working together in order to achieve the correct feeling for each technique is the best and quickest way of learning.

It is better to start with one technique at a time as it is difficult to think about many new judo techniques all at once.

When I am using tai-otoshi, I move my opponent in four basic directions, so that I can first get used to a simple movement and later build up to a complete moving randori practice.

When my partner is moving away from me, it means that I have to move towards him, and to gain the necessary contact I will need a bigger movement. When my partner moves towards me, a much faster turning movement is required. The movement needs to be quicker because I have less time to attack when they move towards me than when they move away from me.

In a tai-otoshi attack, when my opponent is moving away from my left side, the movement is bigger. When my opponent moves in the opposite direction the movement into the tai-otoshi becomes smaller and quicker.

Once you are able to make the different adjustments for the throwing techniques in these basic directions, and all the fundamentals are working together, you can then start a less regimented moving randori. By working with a number of different grips for each technique you can begin to ingrain the throws in order to make the attacks as natural and as easy as possible.

Once you have mastered a number of techniques you can then begin to link them together in your 'loose' randori practice. With this type of practice you rapidly become accustomed to changing the direction of the techniques to suit your opponent's movements.

# Speed uchi-komi

Although speed is important for the execution of techniques, you must be careful when practising fast uchi-komi movements that the quality of the techniques is not lost.

It is very beneficial to your judo to have a good coach monitoring speed uchi-komi training. Too often the mistake is made of trying to do a number of uchi-komi movements within a time limit. This only contributes towards the deterioration of the techniques and the forming of bad habits.

Remember, it is the speed of the individual technique that is important and not the number of techniques that are made in a fixed amount of time.

With all speed-technique training the quality is of utmost importance. Try not to get uchi-komi speed training and endurance training mixed up.

## THREE-MAN UCHI-KOMI – POWER

One of the best ways of increasing the power of your tachi-waza technique without actually completing the throw is by three-man uchi-komi. The third man holds the belt of uke and must ensure that he anchors uke in order that tori can make a 100% attacking movement.

This can be done on the move, but small movements rather than big ones are recommended. If tori is attacking with rear throws the anchor man should put his shoulder against uke's back but ensure that uke's posture is upright. Team work from all three judoka is the key and you must try to adapt to each other's movements.

# *Tachi-waza uchi-komi programme*

It is easy to devise your own uchi-komi programme to suit your own range of techniques and level of physical fitness. Try to experiment a little with your programme to inject some variation.

Here is an example of a simple tachi-waza uchi-komi programme for you to base your own on.

**Uchi-komi fundamentals**

| | |
|---|---|
| Hands, body, legs | 3×20 on each part increasing the number of sets as your condition improves |

**Uchi-komi static techniques**

| | |
|---|---|
| Uchi-mata | 3×10 increasing the sets |
| Osoto-gari | 3×10 increasing the sets |
| Ashi-waza | 3×10 increasing the sets |
| O-uchi-gari | 3×10 increasing the sets |
| Seoi-nage | 3×10 increasing the sets |
| Tai-otoshi | 3×10 increasing the sets |

**Uchi-komi – four basic directions techniques**

| | |
|---|---|
| Uchi-mata | 5× attacks in all four directions |
| Osoto-gari | 5× attacks in all four directions |
| Ashi-waza | 5× attacks in all four directions |
| O-uchi-gari | 5× attacks in all four directions |
| Seoi-nage | 5× attacks in all four directions |
| Tai-otoshi | 5× attacks in all four directions |

**Uchi-komi – randori techniques**

| | | |
|---|---|---|
| Uchi-mata | 3×5 | |
| Osoto-gari | 3×5 | |
| Ashi-waza | 3×5 | These randori uchi-komi do not have to be done in any set order. |
| O-uchi-gari | 3×5 | |
| Seoi-nage | 3×5 | |
| Tai-otoshi | 3×5 | |

Speed uchi-komi should be done in no more than sets of five repetitions. The number of sets will vary according to the individual.

Once the entry into the technique and the individual aspects of the technique have been practised with uchi-komi, the only part left to practise is the completion of the throw. This is called nage-komi.

# Nage-komi – throwing practice

Nage-komi is one of the most neglected parts of technique training in European judo and I feel it is one of the key factors behind the success of the Japanese. The Japanese have the advantage of many judoka to practise with and are taught from an early age the importance of ukemi.

In Japan all the dojos are purpose-built for judo and most of the mats are laid on sprung flooring, which makes falling much less painful. If a mat is hard it is very important to practise controlled nage-komi to ensure your partner does not get injured, and for dynamic throwing techniques a crash mat is essential.

All technique finishing should now be done on the move and in a realistic randori situation. Complete cooperation is needed from both judoka and in order to keep a throwing rhythm it is better to practise nage-komi in a group.

# Nage-komi programme

Nage-komi is best practised at the end of the judo session while you are still warm. If there a number of judoka in the class you can practise by putting a few of them in the middle of the mat and attempting to throw each one five times, changing the techniques all the time.

All of the techniques I have demonstrated in this chapter are for a right-handed attack, but they can and should be practised on the left. Although you will have a favourite side, do not neglect the side that does not feel comfortable. Repetition is the key. The more you do, the easier the techniques become until they are second nature.

## NE-WAZA UCHI-KOMI

Ne-waza uchi-komi is every bit as important as tachi-waza uchi-komi with just as many techniques and variations to be practised, if not more.

The main difficulty with ne-waza uchi-komi is getting a good rhythm with the technique. Team work is of the essence.

As with tachi-waza uchi-komi, ne-waza uchi-komi requires you to build up the fundamentals that make up the individual techniques.

# Osae-komi-waza uchi-komi

One of the best ways to learn osae-komi-waza is to get your partner to lie on their back, then for you to lie across them making sure that you have chest contact with their chest, as in photograph 8a. With a little resistance from your partner, move around their body making sure that you have control at all times of their head and contact with their chest, see photographs 8b, c, d.

For the beginners reading this book: it is important that your partner's legs are avoided throughout this practice. Any entanglement with the legs would result in the osae-komi-waza being broken.

As you change into different positions, again it is a good idea to have a coach instructing you on small technicalities so that the techniques are more effective. There are numerous hand-holds that can be taken and it is up to the individual to experiment with them.

*8a, b, c, d This combination can be done in any order and can be changed to suit your favourite osae-komi-waza*

# Turnovers from the knees

One of the most popular ways of defending in ne-waza is with uke on his hands and knees. This leaves many opportunities for tori to attack, and there is a choice of techniques that he or she can use.

The legs are very important in ne-waza and play a big part in controlling uke throughout an attack. In photographs 9a, b, c, you can see that both my legs are controlling my partner, and in photograph 9c after rolling them over I can now decide whether to turn into an osae-komi-waza, kansetsu-waza or shime-waza.

To ensure that a good uchi-komi rhythm is kept up, make sure that after completing your movements, uke quickly returns to the kneeling position.

*9a, b, c Both my legs are controlling my opponent . . . I roll them over . . . and can decide to turn into an osae-komi-waza, kansetsu-waza or shime-waza*

# Turnovers off the back

Although it might seem from photographs 30a, 30b and 30c on page 42 that the person between the legs is the attacker, this can be a very strong attacking position for the person lying on their back. This shows a simple turnover off the back, which is a very easy technique from which to obtain a rhythm.

Using my legs to control my opponent, and controlling their head, I then force him over into tate-shiho-gatame. A similar turning movement can be used for juji-gatame and sangaku-jime, and there are many other possibilities from this position. Do not be afraid to experiment.

# Ne-waza uchi-komi programme

This is a basic guide for a ne-waza uchi-komi programme but can be changed to suit your individual needs.

**Uchi-komi osae-komi-waza techniques**

| Various techniques moving from one hold to another | 5×2 minutes with your partner giving a little persistence |
|---|---|

**Uchi-komi turnovers from knees techniques**

Turns into osae-komi-waza
|  | (two variations) (a) | 3×10 |
|---|---|---|
|  | (b) | 3×10 |

Turns into kansetsu-waza
|  | (two variations) (a) | 3×10 |
|---|---|---|
|  | (b) | 3×10 |

Turns into shime-waza
|  | (two variations) (a) | 3×10 |
|---|---|---|
|  | (b) | 3×10 |

**Uchi-komi turnovers off the back techniques**

Turns into osae-komi-waza
|  | (two variations) (a) | 3×10 |
|---|---|---|
|  | (b) | 3×10 |

Turns into kansetsu-waza
|  | (two variations) (a) | 3×10 |
|---|---|---|
|  | (b) | 3×10 |

Turns into shime-waza
|  | (two variations) (a) | 3×10 |
|---|---|---|
|  | (b) | 3×10 |

## LIGHT RANDORI

20 minutes (changing partner if possible)

In tachi-waza light randori, the idea is to practise the techniques in a more realistic situation with little resistance from uke. Exactly the same applies for ne-waza and it is possible to practise alternate techniques with your partner if you wish. This is one of the best ways of learning to change from one technique to another, as it is not always the first technique that finishes the contest.

After having practised both tachi-waza and ne-waza techniques separately, you need to consider the importance of linking them together. Many judoka are specialists in tachi-waza and many in ne-waza, but there are very few who are equally skilful in both. It is like being in a gun fight with two pistols and only using one! Only half of your armoury is being used.

It is necessary to practise linking the two together, as in a competitive situation there is only a split second to follow from tachi-waza into ne-waza.

# Example 1: tai-otoshi/juji-gatame

Photographs 10a, b, c, show a very popular combination with the first tachi-waza attack being a tai-otoshi. Not having scored the maximum ippon, I very quickly follow up with a juji-gatame. This is a very easy attacking movement to practise with uchi-komi.

*10a, b, c  These three photographs show a continuous movement from my tai-otoshi into juji-gatame*

# Example 2: tai-otoshi/sangaku-jime

The same situation can apply for this particular combination. This is where cooperation from a good uke is vital. Once you have thrown your partner, get them to turn immediately on to their front and then attack with your ne-waza technique. You are then able to practise whatever combination you wish, whether it is a throw into a turnover, kansetsu-waza or shime-waza.

Set yourself a target of three to five combinations and repeat them at least ten times each. The days of the old uchi-komi routines, where sometimes up to 1000 static repetitions were performed before randori practice, are over. By planning it carefully and making it as interesting as possible, you will find that uchi-komi will improve your judo so much more quickly.

# Fitness for judo

The big question you need to ask when someone proudly proclaims, 'I'm really fit', is 'fit for what?' So much time and effort can be wasted by doing the wrong forms of training at the wrong times. The first thing to consider is what the object of the training is, and then to direct it accordingly. Obviously, a judoka's main aim is to improve his or her judo performance, and therefore the training sessions, whether they are running, weightlifting or judo itself, must complement the final aim.

It is important for a judoka to have a base level of fitness in order to train judo skills properly. This means that less effort is required to sustain prolonged skill-practise sessions without any deterioration of the actual skills.

For good judo condition, the more judo-related training the better. Remember, there is no substitute for judo itself and all other forms of training should only be used to improve the base level of fitness and complement and help in any weaker judo areas. For example, in a country such as Japan, where there are many judoka of a high standard practising in almost every dojo, their judo cardiovascular conditioning is not a problem. But for someone who can only get to a judo club two or three times a week, although the skill fac-

tor may not be a problem because of good judo coaching, with only two or three black belts and a few kyu grades practising, it is very difficult to build up any kind of judo condition without other forms of training to supplement it.

One form of judo condition-training is fast uchi-komi repetition, although this should be carefully supervised by a coach to ensure that the techniques are being performed correctly and are not being lost through speed. See skill training on page 98.

Whatever forms of training are chosen to complement your judo, you must remember that it is very difficult to train the same way throughout the year. Not only is it very boring, but you also become stale. Therefore, at the beginning of every year you should work out a judo calendar and structure your training to reach a peak at certain times throughout the year.

You may decide that you don't want to train like a world champion. However, whatever your standard or ambitions it is better to perform to the best of your ability, and a basic structure to your training makes a considerable difference.

There is real truth in the saying 'A change is as good as a rest', and alternating parts of a training programme will enable you to enjoy your training more fully. After all, whatever your aims are, you must enjoy what you are doing.

For a training judoka there are four components for physical fitness. They are: cardiovascular conditioning, muscular endurance, power and flexibility.

## CARDIOVASCULAR CONDITIONING AND ENDURANCE

This is the ability to continue demanding work and exercise for long periods of time. The efficiency of the cardiovascular system depends on the body's ability to supply oxygen to the working muscles. This is improved when more capillaries (small blood vessels) are developed in the muscles, thus giving a better supply of nutrients and oxygen. Cardiovascular training improves heart and lung efficiency – the heart is able to pump greater quantities of blood around the body and the lungs have a larger capacity which means that more oxygen can be absorbed. The more oxygen the body is able to take in and utilize, the more work the body is capable of doing.

Cardiovascular endurance enables the body to recover rapidly from physical work and this is particularly important to the judoka, especially in competition circumstances.

There are several ways in which cardiovascular endurance training can be done:

randori practise,
cycling,
running,
swimming,
skipping.

Running is one form of cardiovascular conditioning that I would particularly recommend to the judoka (unless there is a medical reason why this is not suitable for you, such as a knee injury) as it exercises you both aerobically and anaerobically. The distance and speed at which you run determine whether you are training aerobically or anaerobically. Initially, you need a base aerobic condition, so slightly longer runs at about 60–70% of maximum are best to achieve this.

## *Aerobic and anaerobic training*

It is possible for a muscle to contract for a time without oxygen, since although oxygen is vital to muscle activity, it is used more in recovering from and preparing for contraction than in releasing energy for contraction. In the absence of oxygen (the anaerobic state), contraction does not continue until all glycogen (a form of glucose which can be stored) is reduced to lactic acid. Contraction is limited by the ability of the tissue to tolerate the lactic acid produced. Some individuals are less tolerant to this acid than others because of differences in the speed at which lactic acid diffuses out of their muscle cells and into their circulation. By accumulating lactic acid, you literally go into debt for oxygen and you must repay that debt at a later time with an increased oxygen uptake.

The ability to incur an oxygen debt is particularly important in short bursts of strenuous exercise. For example, someone might run a 100 metre sprint in about ten seconds; since they usually hold their breath during the run, the entire requirement of about six litres of oxygen becomes an oxygen debt. It is repaid after the race by increased breathing and oxygen consumption until all of the accumulated oxygen debt is repaid.

A heart-lung system which has been improved and trained by exercise for efficiency supplies enough oxygen to enable the glycogen to be reduced to lactic acid in the presence of oxygen (aerobically). Aerobic training would therefore be produced with longer, steadier runs and anaerobic training with short fast shuttle runs. For contest judo, a judoka needs to train both aerobically and anaerobically.

Judo requires immense effort and, therefore, often prevents full oxygenation of the muscles. In contest judo, aerobic training prevents unnecessary oxygen debt and anaerobic training enables energy demand to be met when breathing becomes restricted due to the close contact of judoka in competition.

Obviously, differences in size and stature contribute tremendously to the type of running an individual is most suited to. A heavyweight such as Yamashita at 120 kg would not run as well as a super lightweight like Karen Briggs who only weighs 48 kg. However, although distance is a problem for him because of his weight, his explosive sprinting capacity (anaerobic capacity) is phenomenal: 'I was obviously not as good as the lighter boys on the Japanese squad when it came to the longer distances, but I was one of the fastest over a 60-metre or 100-metre distance.'

His time over 100 metres was a remarkable thirteen seconds and this type of explosive speed was one of Yamashita's biggest advantages over the other heavyweights.

Although he still ran two miles every other day, he thinks that the explosive running, also every other day, was essential for his judo.

For a heavyweight, I would recommend the following running programme:
(a)  1.5–2 miles every other day at 60–70% of maximum.
(b)  60-metre sprints every other day at 90–100% of maximum. These would consist of four sets of 4×60 metres with a brisk walk back to the starting position after each sprint and a brief rest of sixty seconds between each set.

Even if you are not a competition judoka, a base conditioning will help enormously with your judo.

Karen Briggs is one of the fittest judoka in the world and running is a very important part of her training. Known to the judo world as a human dynamo, she has a tremendous work-rate level throughout her contests.

Karen's running programme is different to that of Yamashita: 'I have to concentrate on the conditioning aspect for my judo so I distance-run and swim for my cardiovascular training and do short sprints for my explosive judo. The closer I get to a competition the less distance running I do, so that I can concentrate on my shuttle running for my anaerobic training.'

Karen's running programme would consist of the following:

(a) 3–4 miles at 70–80% maximum every other day. Some days she misses the run and swims instead.

'Sometimes I find running very boring and so I prefer to swim. It is just as beneficial and without the stress on the joints that running can produce.'

(b) Team sprints with the national judo squad when they are all training together before major events. It often helps to train in a group as some judoka find training alone difficult. Training together can be a great motivator and relieves the boredom that individuals sometimes feel when training by themselves.

(c) Shuttle runs consisting of six lengths of 15 metres for each set and six sets, with a rest between each set. This 6×6×15-metre programme would be Karen's basic shuttle programme and she would build up to 10×10×15 metres.

The resting period between each set is determined by the amount of time it takes to run a set. So if, for example, it takes thirty seconds to run a set, this is the length of time you have to rest in between.

Karen shuttle runs from about halfway through an eight-week programme and stops approximately one and a half weeks before the competition.

Shuttle running just before a competition is not advisable as the body needs a few days to recover from hard training. Karen would only do light uchi-komi and suppling in the final week prior to her contest.

## MUSCULAR ENDURANCE

Muscular endurance is the ability of the muscles to perform work continuously. For a judoka it is very important, because fatigue can rapidly set in with all the constant work on particular muscle groups used in judo.

Muscular endurance can be increased by raising the number of repetitions of an exercise to work the muscle groups harder. Weights can be used in this type of training if you have the facilities of a gymnasium, but you can achieve almost the same effect without weights in your own home.

If weights are used they should be kept light as it is not the muscular power that is to be increased but the capacity of the muscles to work continuously.

I have set out two different muscular-endurance circuits, one with and one without weights.

# Muscular endurance programme with weights

**Cleans**  With this exercise your posture is very important and at no time should your back be bent.

The bar is pulled upwards from a standing position until it reaches the chest. It must then be lowered, with control, back down to the floor.

Repetitions: 3×10 building to 3×15.

This exercise is particularly good for the legs and the pulling action essential for judo.

**Inclined sit-ups** (bent legs)  For this exercise you need an inclined sit-up bench with something to anchor your feet under. During the sit-ups you must keep your midsection in contact with the bench and your hands behind your neck.

From a lying position (bent leg) sit up until your elbows touch your knees.

Repetitions: 3×15 building to 3×30.

As you get better you can also increase the incline of the bench.

**Half-squats**   Once again, posture is very important with this exercise and the back should be kept straight with the head held up at all times.

Use something soft to cushion your neck when you place a light weight behind it.

As it is very important not to put unecessary stress on the knees during this exercise, place a bench between your legs. As you squat, bend your knees until your bottom touches the bench. The bench will ensure that the legs do not bend more than the 90° angle necessary.

Repetitions: 3×10 building to 3×20.

**Curls**   Keep the back straight to avoid any unnecessary pressure on it.

Take an underhand grip on the bar and curl the bar up to your chest, then lower it back to the starting position.

Repetitions: 3×10 building up to 3×20.

**Hanging knees to chest** For this exercise you need a chinning bar to hang from. Although it is an abdominal exercise it is one of the best methods of improving your judo grips. As you hang from the bar your own body weight pulls on the fingers and works the forearms.

For the second part of this exercise, bring your knees up to your chest and then lower to the starting position and repeat.

Repetitions: 3×10 building up to 3×20.

**Quads** Many judoka have problems with their knees, so this exercise is particularly important for strengthening the legs. It works on the quadriceps (major muscles in the thigh).

From a sitting position with a fixed load or weight attached to either the ankles or lower part of the leg by means of appropriate apparatus in the gymnasium, straighten the legs to take the load, bend and then repeat.

Repetitions: 3×10 building up to 3×20.

**Upward rows** Excellent for the judoka as they improve the pulling action required for judo. They also strengthen the fingers and forearms.

Take an overhand grip on the bar with hands approximately shoulder-width apart and pull your body upwards to your chin.

Repetitions: 3×10 building up to 3×15.

**Inclined leg-raises** Lie on an inclined bench with your head at the highest point. Grip wallbars (in most gyms they should be behind your head; if not, make sure there is something solid to hold on to) and then raise your legs until they reach your head. At all times during this exercise your legs should be straight and your feet together. Gently lower your legs until they almost touch the bench and then repeat. It is important to do this slowly so that you have perfect control and your feet don't touch the bench.

Repetitions: 3×10 building up to 3×20.

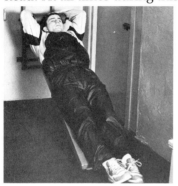 

**Bench step-ups** A bench or chair approximately 45 cm high is required. The seat-height of the chair obviously varies depending on the height of the person, but your legs should not bend more than 90° during the exercise.

Put a weight behind your neck (not too heavy), cushioned to make it more comfortable, and then step up on to the bench and down again using alternate legs. When you are standing on the bench, make sure that the leg is straight.

Repetitions: 25 building up to 30 on each leg.

For maximum effect with this circuit it is important to try and do it at least three times a week.

# Local muscular endurance circuit without weights

For this circuit the body is divided into three sections:

(**a**) upper body – chest, triceps and biceps
(**b**) middle body – abdomen and back
(**c**) lower body – legs

There are nine different exercises in this circuit, three in each section.

The circuit should be repeated three times so that you are doing a total of twenty-seven exercises. You should go from one exercise to another until all nine are completed, so that each section of the body is worked in turn. This also ensures that each section does not become too fatigued.

At no time during this local endurance circuit should you rest, unless of course you feel faint.

**Push-ups** Push-ups should be done with a straight back and the midsection of the body must not touch the floor during the exercise.

Repetitions: 10 building up to 30 for advanced.

**Bent-leg sit-ups** Anchor your feet under something secure (a sofa will do if you are exercising at home) and clasp your hands behind your neck. Sit up until your elbows touch your knees. At no time let your bottom lift off the floor during the exercise.

Repetitions: 20 building up to 50.

**Star jumps** From a crouching position, spring upwards into a standing star shape.

Repetitions: 10 building up to 25.

**Tricep dips** For this exercise you will need two chairs a small distance apart. Place your feet on one chair and your hands on the other and dip down between the chairs by bending your elbows as far as you can go. Straighten your arms and repeat.

Repetitions: 15 building up to 40

**Dorsal raises** Lie flat on your front with your face towards the floor and your arms out to either side of you. Lift your legs and upper body simultaneously – your mid-section remains in contact with the floor.

Repetitions: 10 building up to 25.

**Squat thrusts**   Start this exercise from the push-up position. Bring your knees up towards your chest until they touch your elbows, so that you are squatting, and then return to the push-up position.
Repetitions: 20 building to 50.

**Chins** (under- or over-arm)   For this exercise you will need a bar to hang from. It should be higher than your fully extended body.

Take an under- or over-hand grip on the bar and pull your body upwards until your chin passes over the bar, then slowly lower yourself, with control, back down until your arms are straight.
Repetitions: 5 building up to 20.

**V-ups**   In this exercise your midsection should stay in contact with the floor throughout. Start from a lying position with your arms above your head and your legs firmly together. Simultaneously raise your upper body and legs until they form a V with your body.
Repetitions: 10 building up to 25.

**Bench step-ups**   These are done in exactly the same way as the step-ups in the alternative muscular endurance circuit (page 114), but with weights held in the hands (these vary depending on the size of the person doing the exercise, but should not be too heavy).
Repetitions: 25 building up to 30 on each leg.

# POWER (STRENGTH) TRAINING

Strength can be developed by either isotonic or isometric exercises.

Isometric exercises produce a muscle contraction in which the muscle develops tension but does not shorten. The disadvantage of isometric exercises for judo is that they only develop strength at one point in the range of movement. In a sport with all the varying techniques to be performed, it is much more beneficial to do isotonic exercises.

Isotonic exercises produce a muscle contraction in which the muscle is allowed to shorten and lift a load and thus do work. Therefore, to improve power with isotonic exercises you need few repetitions against a high resistance. Too much power training is not good for judo and I personally never stayed on this section of training for more than two weeks in the middle of a six to eight week build-up for a major competition.

I feel that the heavier judo competitors, such as Yamashita and Parisi, benefit more from a power programme than a middleweight like myself, or a lighter weight like Karen Briggs, because their judo tends to be more static (although no less dynamic) when performing their techniques.

However, I feel that for most judoka a muscular endurance programme is more beneficial than a power programme.

The pyramid system is the most effective way of building power.

You start your first set with a fixed load and perform eight repetitions, then increase the weight and decrease the repetitions by two at a time.

Finish by doing one exercise at maximum effort.

# SUPPLING AND MOBILITY

Suppling and mobility exercises are different, and it is important that you know the differences before using them in your training programme.

Suppling exercises are 'passive' in nature. They slowly stretch muscles to their maximum range, and the muscle is held there. These exercises aim at extending the maximum active range of a skilled movement within the limits of the structure and function of the joint. This can decrease the possibility of injury by increasing the stress-resistance factor of the joint.

Mobility exercises are 'ballistic', i.e. with movement, and they are used as part of the warm-up. They cause muscles to tighten up. Here you work well within the maximum range.

Passive suppling is, I think, the most useful form for the judoka, because once exercises become ballistic, there is a real danger of being injured for someone who doesn't really know what they are doing. For example, many times I've seen people 'bouncing' a suppling exercise, which is totally wrong. The natural reaction of a trained muscle when encountering a sudden movement is to tighten up in order to prevent the muscle being damaged – so when your muscle is wrongly being pushed past its maximum range in this situation, it can tighten and then rip.

It is absolutely imperative for all judoka to have a suppling programme to follow and keep to religiously. So many times you see muscle-bound fighters who can't put their arms behind their necks – these are inevitably the ones who suffer later. It is important with all suppling exercises that you relax in the set position for a period of time. The amount of time spent in each position will, of course, determine just how supple you will be.

Think of your body being in three different sections: legs, midsection and arms. Each section should be stretched in three particular directions: forwards, backwards and sideways. This way, all muscle groups are suppled: the prime movers (muscles that positively contract to affect the direction of the movement), antagonists (muscles that apply a degree of contraction in the opposite direction, affecting the quality of the movement) and fixators (the muscles which contract in order to ensure a stability in all related joints and in the direction of the movement).

The following programme is one that can be practised alone, as opposed to in suppling pairs. The first exercise in each section is in fact ballistic, and should be used to warm up the muscles. (Be careful not to take the joints and muscles anywhere near your maximum active range.)

# Legs
## Hip girdle

**Leg swinging**  This prepares the hip joint for the actual suppling which is to follow. Swing forwards, backwards and sideways, and do so in an upright position, with the leg that is not swinging remaining at all times straight, and with the heel on the ground.

A wall bar, or any fixture about waist-high, can be held for extra balance. At least ten times on each leg in each direction is necessary.

**Forward**  Stand sideways to the wall and swing the outside leg, keeping it straight, towards the chest.

**Backward**  Stand at arm's length, facing the wall, and swing the leg backwards while bending forward slightly at the waist.

**Sideways**  Stand in the same position facing the wall. Now, take the swinging leg across the body and swing it upward and to the side, keeping the hips facing the wall.

# Hamstrings (back of the thigh)

Sit either in a hurdle position, or with both legs held together and straight, and attempt to lower your stomach on to your thighs. Keep your head up at all times and lower yourself until you feel your hamstrings tighten. Hold the position for thirty seconds on each leg and repeat three times.

## Hamstrings/quadriceps

**Forward splits**  Splits is an ideal suppling exercise for the judoka. Straighten both legs, forward and backwards, and lower your body gently and as far as possible. Keep the trunk and head upright and hold on to something for extra stability. Hold for ten seconds and repeat three times.

**Box splits**  Stand square to a wall bar and slide both legs out sideways until maximum range is reached. At all times, keep both legs straight and your hips forward. Hold for twenty seconds and repeat three times.

**Tai-otoshi box splits**  Exactly the same position as above should be taken. Then, once full range in the box split has been obtained, simply rotate firstly your right hip and then your left hip forward and hold for twenty seconds. Repeat three times.

# *Midsection*

## Hip rotation

A ballistic movement to warm up the midsection. Simply rotate your hips in a circular movement, first to the left side and then the right side, and repeat – three lots of ten times on each side.

**Twisting hip rotation**  A suppling exercise. Lie face down with your arms in a crucifix position. Now take firstly the left leg across your back and place it on the floor as close to your right arm as possible. The more supple ones can grip the foot in order to place it as high up on the opposite side as possible.

At all times, keep the hips in contact with the floor in order to isolate the rotation of the hip. Now repeat this on the opposite side. Hold the position for twenty seconds and repeat three times both on the left and the right.

# Arms

## Arm swinging

A ballistic exercise is necessary to warm up the shoulder joints.

Swing both arms in a large circular movement, keeping as close to your body as possible. Ten full swings forwards and backwards should warm up the joints ready for suppling.

Once again, there are three directions in which we supple the arms and shoulders and they are a) when the arms are held straight backwards over the head, b) when the arms are taken from a position at the side, backwards and upwards to the rear, and c) when the upper arm is rotated upwards and across behind the neck.

**Backwards above the head**  Use a wall bar at about waist height and take a grip a shoulder-width apart on the bar. Now bend forward at the waist so that your arms and back form a straight line. Keeping the arms straight, bend hard at the waist until your maximum shoulder range is reached. Hold for thirty seconds and repeat.

**Behind back**  Sit on the floor with your arms stretched out behind you and your hands as close together as possible. Slide forward, holding your head up until you reach your maximum range. Maintain for thirty seconds and repeat three times.

**Upwards and across behind the neck** This exercise can be done either sitting down or standing.

Put the arm that is to be suppled across the back of the neck, keeping your head forward. Using the other arm, take a firm grip of your elbow and, keeping the arm being suppled relaxed, pull the elbow across and towards the other shoulder until maximum range is reached. Maintain for thirty seconds and repeat three times.

# The aims and rules of competition judo

Everyone has different reasons for practising sport, but the main aim should always be to enjoy what you are doing. Many judoka prefer the technical and philosophical side of the sport as opposed to the hard competition side. Both, however, are important in their own ways.

The problem with many competition judoka is that they neglect the complexities of the techniques. Therefore the need to study cannot be emphasized enough. OK, so it could be argued that the main aim of judo is to score an ippon. But what is more important is the way in which it's obtained.

## SCORES

## *Ippon*

An ippon is the equivalent of a knockout in boxing and can be achieved in four different ways. An ippon scores ten points, and as soon as it is achieved the contest is over.

### Nage-komi-waza (the throw)

This is where a person is thrown with 'impetus' on his or her back, and can be done with a number of techniques varying in the three basic directions: forwards, backwards and sideways. The different techniques that can be used to throw are too numerous to mention. The examples shown in this book are some of the best ippon throws that you are likely to see.

*Divisenko of the Soviet Union defeats Neueuther of West Germany with a leaping sambo-style armlock (1983 European Championships)*

## Osae-komi-waza (the hold-down)

The main aim of the osae-komi-waza is to 'pin' your opponent on his or her back or at least three-quarters of it, for the duration of thirty seconds. Osae-komi-waza vary, but as long as there is not entanglement of the legs, and sufficient contact and control of your opponent, the thirty-second countdown commences.

## Kansetsu-waza (the armlock, or joint technique)

There are two types of kansetsu-waza that can be applied for a submission hold. One is juji-gatame which is pressure against the joint when the arm is completely locked, and the other is ude-garami which involves the twisting of the arm joints. Both techniques result in a submission which is acknowledged with either a tap on the opponent's body or on to the mat. The kansetsu-waza, like the shime-waza, is a very specialized movement, and is one of my favourite specialities.

## Shime-waza (the strangle)

As with the kansetsu-waza, the shime-waza can finish the contest with a submission hold. Once again there are numerous variations, but the two basic ways of applying a shime-waza are with the arms and hands, or with the legs.

When a shime-waza is being applied with the arms and hands there are two pressure points on the neck. The first is the windpipe. When pressure is applied here it prevents the air supply reaching the

*I armlock Kase of Japan to win the world title (1981 World Championships)*

*Angelo Parisi throws his Swiss opponent for ippon with seoi-otoshi (1979 European Championships)*

lungs. This is known as a hadaka-jime, or choke, because no part of the judo jacket is used in its application. See example.

The second pressure point is the jugular vein, which cuts off the blood supply to the brain. See example.

When a shime-waza is applied with the legs, tori must have control of both uke's arm and neck.

As in all sports, the ultimate aim is not always possible, so there are often only minor scores at the end of the five-minute contest period. The one with the highest score is the winner. The points are not cumulative, except for the waza-ari. Minor scores are given when throwing techniques or hold-downs do not produce an ippon. These minor scores are called waza-ari, yuko and koka and given seven, five and three points respectively.

# Waza-ari

This seven-point score is given when an opponent is thrown on to their side with impetus. A waza-ari is almost an ippon and if a player scores two of them they count as an ippon score and the contest ends. Waza-ari are the only scores which can be added to make an ippon. A waza-ari can also be scored when an osae-komi-waza hold-down lasts twenty-five or more seconds, but does not make the thirty-second limit needed for an ippon.

# Yuko

This five-point score is awarded for a near waza-ari when an opponent has been thrown with less impetus on their side. It is also given for an osae-komi-waza lasting between twenty and twenty-four seconds. There is no limit to the number of yukos

127

that can be gained in a five-minute contest period. For example, if at the end of a contest one player has five yuko scores and the other player has four yuko scores, the one with the most yukos would win by a five-point score.

*I attack Nagysolymosi of Hungary (1982 European Championships)*

# Koka

This three-point score is awarded if the opponent is tripped on to any part of his or her underside (rear), but not necessarily with much force. It is also awarded after the duration of fifteen seconds in an osae-komi-waza.

A koka is the lowest possible score and any higher score would override it. For example, if at the end of a contest one player has one yuko and the other player has five kokas, the person with the yuko wins.

## PENALTIES

There are three different penalty points which may be given. They are called shido, chui and keikoku, and they give three, five and seven points respectively. During a contest, awarding a penalty is at the judge's discretion.

Any score from a throwing technique or an osae-komi-waza overrides the equivalent score of a penalty. Penalty points are awarded to your opponent.

# Shido

There are a number of ways in which the three-point penalty can be awarded. the most common reason for a shido is when there has been no positive attack made by a competitor for at least twenty seconds. When this happens, before the penalty is awarded the referee gives a warning (passivity warning) to the guilty player or players by a turning over of the hands. (It is possible for both judoka to be awarded a shido at the same time.) If a further twenty seconds elapses with a positive attack the referee then awards the shido.

There are many other minor infringements of the rules for which the shido penalty is given. They are as follows:

(a) An extreme jigotai
(b) i Holding the opponent's collar, lapel or jacket on the same side with both hands;
ii holding the bottom of the opponent's jacket with both hands, i.e. below the belt line;
iii holding one sleeve of the opponent's jacket with both hands.
(c) Continually holding the opponent's sleeves while in a standing position for defensive purposes.
(d) Inserting a finger or fingers inside the opponent's sleeve or bottom of their trousers.

(e) In a standing position, continually keeping the fingers of one or both of the opponent's hands interlocked to prevent the continuation of the contest.
(f) Disarranging his or her judo-gi intentionally.
(g) Encircling the belt or jacket around any part of the opponent's body.
(h) Putting a hand, arm, foot or leg directly on the opponent's face.
(i) From a standing position, taking hold of the opponent's feet, legs or trousers with the hands, unless simultaneously attempting a throwing technique.

# Chui

This is a five-point penalty and more serious than the shido. A chui is given to a competitor for an important infringement of the rules, or when a shido is upgraded for a second minor infringement. For example, a shido passivity penalty is upgraded to a chui if a further twenty seconds elapse without a proper attack.

The referee may award a chui for any of the following infringements;

(a) Applying dojime (scissors with the legs) to the opponent's trunk, neck or head.

(b) Kicking the opponent with a knee or foot in order to release their grip.
(c) Bending back an opponent's fingers in order to break their grip.
(d) Pulling an opponent down into newaza without attempting a proper technique first.
(e) From a standing position, going outside the contest area while applying a technique which has been started inside the mat area.
(f) Intentionally going outside the contest area or intentionally forcing the opponent to go outside the contest area.

# Keikoku

This is a seven-point penalty. It is given if there has been a grave infringement of the rules or if a chui has already been given

and the player commits a further minor or major infringement. If a player is awarded a keikoku in a contest, he or she is disqualified if any other penalty is given.

A referee may also award a keikoku if a player:

(**a**) Attempts to throw the opponent by winding one of their legs around that of their opponent while facing in the same direction as them and falling backwards on to them.

(**b**) Applies kansetsu-waza anywhere other than the elbow joint.

(**c**) Lifts a player into the air when they are lying on their back and drives them into the mat.

(**d**) Sweeps an opponent's legs away from the inside while the opponent is attempting a throw such as harai-goshi, etc.

(**e**) Applies any technique or action which might injure the opponent's neck or spinal column (vertebrae).

(**f**) Attempts any technique outside the mat area.

(**g**) Disregards and ignores any of the referee's instructions.

(**h**) Makes any unnecessary remarks or gestures to an opponent.

(**i**) Applies any technique which will endanger the opponent, such as waki-gatame (where a player falls on to the mat while applying a kansetsu-waza).

(**j**) Dives headfirst into the mat while attempting to perform throws such as uchi-mata or harai-goshi. This is a rule which protects tori as it is extremely dangerous and the impact on the head and neck when landing can injure or even kill a competitor.

(**k**) Intentionally falls backwards while an opponent is clinging to their back.

(**l**) Wears any kind of hard or metallic object (covered or not).

# MAT AREA

In judo there are different sizes of mat area just as there are different sizes of rings in boxing. The minimum area is 14 m × 14 m and the maximum area is 16 m × 16 m. All areas are square in shape and have a standard red perimeter line of 1 m around the edge. Penalties can be incurred if a player intentionally steps out of the mat area or if they push their opponent out of the area deliberately. If during a contest the players accidentally step outside the perimeter line, the contest is immediately stopped and resumed again by bringing the players back into the centre of the mat.

A free zone (safety zone) of 2 m must surround the contest mat area.

# CONTEST DURATION

A contest lasts for five minutes unless an 'ippon' is scored, in which case the contest immediately finishes. Whenever there is a break in the contest (e.g. to bring the play-

*I attempt to armlock Kruger of East Germany (1979 World Championships)*

ers back to the centre of the mat), the clock is stopped and then restarted when the referee and contestants are ready. This ensures the full five minutes are fought.

## INJURY TIME

In the past a five-minute injury time was permitted, which meant that if a person was quite badly injured they could receive medical help at regular intervals. This meant, of course, that the contest had to be stopped, and the match became long and disjointed. It was also abused by play-ers who used the injury time for much-needed rests.

Now that injury time has been abolished, it is amazing to see some of the rapid recoveries made by players, although of course genuine injuries still occur.

131

If a contestant is injured and cannot carry on fighting, the contest is awarded to the other player. However, if the injury is caused by the opponent the referee allows medical help so that the contest can continue. If the injured person is considered unfit to continue, the contest can be awarded to them if the referee considers the other person guilty of purposely inflicting the injury.

# THE REFEREE

The referee generally stays within the contest area and ensures that at all times his decisions are correctly recorded. The referee also makes sure that there are no spectators, supporters or photographers in a position to cause a nuisance or risk to the competitors, who will wear either a red or white belt so that the referee can distinguish between them.

# JUDGES

The referee is assisted by two line judges sitting diagonally opposite each other at two corners outside the contest area. If during a competition the referee expresses an opinion which is of a higher degree than that of either of the two judges, he must adjust his evaluation to that of the judge who expressed the higher score. For example, if the referee gives an ippon but the two judges give a waza-ari and a yuko, the referee must give the waza-ari, as it is the higher of the judge's scores.

However, if the referee awards a lower score than that of the two judges, he must use the lower of the two judge's scores. If the referee gives a yuko and one of the judges a waza-ari and the other an ippon, the referee must give a waza-ari. Finally, if the two judges award one score higher and one score lower than that of the referee, the referee may keep his opinion. For example, if one judge awards a waza-ari and the other judge awards a koka, but the referee gives a yuko, then the referee's decision is kept.

At all times the judges should command their corners and indicate to the referee if an action was inside or outside the contest area.

Each judge has two flags, one red and the other white (corresponding to the players' belts). If at the end of the contest there is no score, the referee will call 'Hantei' and the two judges will simultaneously hold up one of their flags indicating which competitor they consider to have won. If their decisions are the same, then the competitor with that colour belt wins. However, if their decisions are different the referee must make the final decision. (This is referred to as a split decision.) If there has been no score, the competitor considered to have made the most positive attacks during the contest is the winner.

# Referees' terminology

Judo originated in Japan in 1880 and to this day remains one of the few sports to have kept its original terminology. One advantage, of course, is that this gives judoka throughout the world an international language which is both convenient and efficient for international relations.

Listed below is the referee's terminology. On page 139 you will find a glossary of judo terms, which is not intended to be a comprehensive dictionary, but a guide to cover most judo circumstances.

**Hajime** (begin). Normally called to start ▶ a competition.

**Matte** (break). Called when the contestants are out of the contest area or if the competition has to be temporarily stopped. The referee signals this command by putting his hand directly in front of himself and towards the timekeepers. ▶

**Sona-mama** (freeze, or don't move). ▶ Normally called when the referee is finding it difficult to see what the two competitors are doing. Generally this happens when two players are entangled and a judo-gi is over one or the other's face. Once the competitors have been separated the referee will then resume the contest. To call sona-mama the referee bends over the two contestants and firmly touches them with both hands while using the command.

**Yoshi** (carry on). The command used to ▶ resume the contest. Any movement from either of the players before yoshi has been called could result in a penalty being given. The referee will restart the contest by applying pressure to the contestants before issuing the command to carry on.

**Sore-made** (finish). Called to indicate the end of the contest. As with hajime, no hand signal is used, only a strong verbal command.

**Toketa** (broken). When a player escapes from an osae-komi-waza in ne-waza the referee calls out toketa because the technique has been broken. This means that the thirty-second countdown stops immediately. The referee indicates this from a standing position and waves one arm from side to side.

**Waza-ari.** Indicated by the referee from a ▶ standing position with one arm at a 90° angle to his or her body.

**Osae-komi** (holding). Called by the referee when a recognized hold has been obtained by either competitor. It is indicated by the referee bending over the fighters with one arm pointed towards them at an approximate 45° angle, and it initiates the time-count.

◀ **Ippon.** The maximum score indicates the end of the contest. The referee calls ippon and simultaneously holds one hand above his head from a standing position.

**Yuko.** Indicated from a standing position with the referee's arm at approximately a 45° angle to the floor.

**Koka.** Indicated by the referee in a ▶ standing position with his or her arm bent and the hand flattened.

**Waza-ari awasete ippon** (two half- ▶ points). Called when a second half-point is scored, and thus added to make a full point. The referee signals a waza-ari with his or her arm, which then changes to the ippon movement by bringing the arm to the chest and then extending the arm above his or her head.

**Wind up.** A warning by the referee to the fighters to take more action. This is done by rotating his hands in front of him and pointing to the judoka concerned.
▼

◀ **Shido/chui/keikoku.** Penalties are given by the referee from a standing position with an outstretched arm and a finger pointing to the player. The referee would not turn his or her body to face the player involved.

**Sogo-gachi, kiken-gachi, fusen-gachi** (winning form). These are called by the referee, depending on which scores override each other. When the referee indicates a winner of a contest by any of these, he or she raises one hand, palm in, above shoulder height towards the winner.

135

**Hansoku-make** (disqualification). The ►
referee, in the event of a disqualification,
returns both players to their starting positions and steps forward between them,
turning to the one being disqualified. The
referee then announces honsoku-make.

**Hantei** (make your decisions). If the contest produces no score, the referee has to
call on the line judges to make their
decisions. This is done by the referee
raising an arm above the head with the
hand facing inward and the command
being called.

**Hiki-wake** (draw). Hiki-wake can only
be scored in a team competition and not
with individual contests. In a team match
when there is no score the referee calls
hiki-wake to indicate a draw. The two line
judges cross their red and white flags and
the referee brings his or her hand from
above the head to directly in front of himself and in between the two contestants.
▼

◄ **Adjust your dress.** In competition the
judo-gi often becomes disarranged, and
after matte is called, the referee can
instruct the fighters to adjust their jackets.

# *Summary*

Whatever sport you choose to follow you must find it enjoyable. Through all my judo years, and some of them have been hard competitively, I have always derived immense pleasure from my sport. I felt the time was right to retire from competitive judo when I began to lose this enjoyment, but after a two-year rest, I discovered that my enthusiasm had rekindled, so I decided to come back. But I did find that I enjoyed judo just as much as a teacher as a competitor.

Too often in modern-day sport great pressures are put upon sportsmen and women to win and to obtain the financial rewards that go with winning. I feel there is something to learn from the words of Pierre de Coubertin, the father of the modern Olympic movement, 'It's not the winning, it's the taking part', which was his modern Olympic ideal. Although the values of winning have changed, and quite rightly, we must not forget the connotations of his statement.

Not everyone is going to be an Olympic champion, or would want to be, and every practising judoka is able to get something different out of the sport. However, I have not met a judoka yet who doesn't want to improve his or her judo, and the rate of progression is up to the individual with the help and guidance of a good coach and some willing partners.

Judo is a neverending learning process and, after twenty-two years' involvement in the sport already, I feel that I have only just scratched the surface. I hope that I have covered many aspects in this book which will help you with your judo in one way or another. A book, of course, is not the perfect training aid, but it can act as a fundamental guide for you, although the real work will start in the dojo itself.

I feel that the history and origin of judo should never be forgotten and should be studied by *all* judoka.

I have not covered kata in this book and the reason for this is that kata is a whole subject within itself and deserves more than just a brief explanation.

The kata are Jigoro Kano's original conceptions of judo performed in what could be described as ritual sequences. Many modern competition judoka have never studied the kata in great length and look on them as a little old-fashioned and even a waste of time. This is one of the unfortunate things about thinking of judo as 'only a sport'.

Someone of Kano's intellect would have had a reason for even some of the more 'outlandish' kata that we find difficult to understand. It would have been interesting to see Kano's interpretation of modern-day judo.

Judo will change over the next hundred years, just as it has done since Kano's day. We have to change with it, but also to try to remember our origins.

As for the future of judo, only time will tell. Certainly the Olympic judo of today is different to the original conception of a hundred years ago. If athletes are to make it to the top of their sports they certainly need to be provided for financially. This also means that the coaches and coaching facilities have to be of a high standard, and a properly structured squad system is imperative for training an élite.

The clubs, though, are where it all begins; this is where all the top judoka started and where the 'crème de la crème' of the future will be found. The two nights a week in an old wooden shack are becoming rarer these days as purpose-built dojos become more and more numerous. Without judo at grassroots level, and by that I mean the clubs, the Yamashitas of the future will not exist.

Japan laid the foundations for judo and the rest of the world has followed. In the 1950s, when the Japanese held the first World Championships, judo was considered an oriental art and the Japanese reigned supreme. Now it is a truly internationally acclaimed sport, practised by millions of people everywhere. I think Kano would be proud of the progress his Kodokan Judo has made throughout the world, and that it is now accepted within education systems everywhere.

It is interesting to see that the Japanese have begun to adopt European training methods and are incorporating forms of weight training into their everyday training routines.

We have advanced so much with the range of techniques and scientific methods of training in our judo, that I feel the open-weight category competitions which have been held in Japan for decades will eventually fade away. I think it is now accepted that a good little one will not beat a good big one.

Some traditions are very hard to change, though, and all we can do is change with the times, keep an open mind and look forward to the next hundred years of judo.

# *Glossary of judo terms*

**Aiki** A form of self-defence based on special principles (lit. harmony of spirit)

**Aikido** The way of Aiki

**Aite** Opponent, partner

**Ao** (Pronounced 'ah-oh') facing up

**Arashi** Storm (yama-arashi, mountain storm)

**Ashi-guruma** Leg wheel

**Ashi-waza** Leg or foot technique

**Atama** Head

**Ate** Strike, hit, punch or kick

**Atemiwaza** Striking techniques using hand, elbow, knee, foot, etc.

**Ayumi-ashi** Normal walking, foot movement

**Bo-jutsu** Stick or staff fighting

**Bu** Martial or military

**Bushi** A knight of feudal Japan

**Butsu-kari** *See* Uchi-komi

**Chiisai** Small

**Chikara** Strength

**Chui** Penalty (equivalent to five points)

**Dan** Step; a black belt grade

**De (v. Deru)** To come out, to advance (de-ashi-harai, advancing sweeping ankle)

**Do** (a) Way, path, etc. This word was frequently used in Chinese and Japanese philosophy in the sense of the way of performing an act in the moral and ethical sense as well as the simple physical. Professor Kano 'borrowed' it from these sources. (b) Trunk of the body

**Dojo** Hall or room in which judo is practised

**Eri** Collar, of a jacket

**Fusegi-kata** Method, form, of defending

**Fusegu** To defend

**Gake (v. kakeru)** To hand, hook, block

**Garami (v. garamu)** To entangle, wrap, bend

**Gari (v. karu)** To reap, as with a scythe

**Gashu-ku** Judo students lodging together for training

**Garame** *see* katame

**Genki** Energetic, lively, active

**Gokyo** The forty basic tachi-waza/throwing techniques

**Gono-kata** Forms of strength

**Gono-sen-no-kata** Forms of counter techniques

**Go-shin-jutsu** The art of self-protection (in all its forms)

**Gyaku** Reverse, upside down (gyaku-juji-jime; fingers-only strangle)

**Ha** Wing

**Hadaka** Naked (hadaka-jime; naked strangle)

**Hairi-kata** The way of entering (for a technique)

**Hajime** Begin.

**Hane** Spring (hane-goshi, spring hip; hane-makikomi, winding throw)

**Hansoku-make** Loss by disqualification

**Hantei** Judgement which the referees call at the end of a drawn contest, calling on the two corner judges to indicate whom they consider to be the winner

**Hara** Stomach

**Harai (barai) (v. harau)** To clear away, sweep (harai-goshi, sweeping loin throw; harai-harai-makikomi, winding throw; harai-tsuri-komi-ashi, propping ankle throw)

**Hidari** Left side

**Hiji** Elbow (hiji-ate, to hit with the elbow)

139

**Hiki (v. hiku)** To pull (hiki-wake, draw)

**Hishige (v. hishigeru)** To crush, squash, smash

**Hiza** Knee (hiza-guruma, knee wheel)

**Hon** (a) Basic. (b) Number suffix for counting long cylindrical objects, therefore: ippon-seoi-nage, one-arm shoulder throw (hon-kami-shiho-gatame, upper four quarters hold; hon-kesa-gatame, basic scarf hold; hon-yoko-shiho-gatame, side four quarters hold)

**Ippon** One point (score value of ten points)

**Ippon-seoi-nage** Shoulder throw

**Itsutsu-no-kata** Forms of five (the five elements/principles)

**Ji** A Japanese ideograph

**Jigotai** Defensive posture

**Jikan** Time (time out)

**Jita-kyoei** The principle that individual advancement benefits society as a whole

**Joseki** The place in the dojo or hall where the seniors or VIPs sit

**Ju** (a) Soft and gentle. This word is taken from Taoist philosophy and embodies the opposite of hard, extreme, unreasonable. Hence the use of 'ju' in judo does not imply soft (as a synonym of easy), but rather reasonable, efficient. Physical action in judo is not meant to be easy (weak) so much as economic. By using the body to its best advantage and exploiting the weaknesses of the opponent, maximum effect can be obtained with maximum efficiency. (b) Ten

**Judo** An Olympic sport, art, combat which is derived from the ancient arts of ju-jitsu by the founder Professor Jigoro Kano

**Judo-gi** The clothes worn when practising or competing at judo. They consist of jacket, trousers and belt. The trousers and jacket are white in colour

**Judoka** A high-grade judo player, but this word is used in the West to describe anybody who practises judo

**Juji-gatame** Straight armlock

**Ju-jitsu (ju-jutsu, jiu-jitsu)** A name covering many forms of close combat in Japan

**Ju-no-kata** The forms of 'gentleness', or simple kata

**Jushin** Centre of gravity for someone or something

**Kaeshi (Gaeshi)** In judo this means 'counter' (e.g. osoto-gaeshi, major outer counter).

**Kake** The point of the throw, the point of maximum power

**Kai (kwai)** society, club

**Kaku (Gaku)** An angle

**Kami** (a) Upper, top. (b) Paper. (c) God(s)

**Kamiza** Upper seat, similar to joseki

**Kansetsu** A joint (of the body)

**Kansetsu-waza** A joint technique armlock

**Kao** Face

**Karate** Empty-handed. A system of fighting without weapons, striking with the hands, feet, elbows etc.

**Karui** Light in weight

**Kata** (a) Form. A training method used in judo and most martial arts. A drill. (b) One of a pair (kata-ha-jime, one-wing strangle). (c) Shoulder ( kata-guruma, shoulder wheel)

**Kata-juji-jime** Fingers and thumb strangle

**Katai** Hard

**Katame (gatame) (v. katemeru)** To harden, tighten, hold (kata-gatame, shoulder hold)

**Katsu (or kappo)** Methods of resuscitation

**Keiko** Practice

**Keikoku** A severe penalty given by the referee (equivalent to seven points)

**Kempo** A method of fighting similar to ju-jitsu

**Ken** Sword

**Kendo** The 'way' of the sword (Japanese two-handed fencing)

**Kendogu** Equipment used for practising kendo

**Keru** To kick (keri-waza, kicking technique)

**Kesa** A Buddhist monk's surplice, worn diagonally across the body. The technique called kesa-gatame means scarf hold

**Ki** Psychic energy

**Kiai** A shout used to harden the body and strengthen the will when maximum effort is required

**Kime (v. kakeru)** To decide

**Kimeno-kata** Forms of decision, which is the kata of self-protection

**Kiri (v.kiru)** To cut, as with a knife

**Ko** (a) Small, minor (ko-uchi-gari, minor inner reaping). (b) Old, ancient

**Kodakan** The headquarters of judo in Japan (Tokyo), the founders' dojo

**Koka** A score, almost a yuko (value three points)

**Koshi (goshi)** Hips (koshi-waza, hip techniques; koshi-jime, hip strangle; koshi-guruma, hip wheel)

**Koshika-no-kata** The kata of ancient forms with techniques suitable for people in armour

**Kosoto-gake** Major outer reaping

**Kosoto-gari** Minor outer reaping

**Kubi** Neck

**Kumikata** The method of grappling of two contestants

**Kuruma (guruma)** (a) Wheel (o-guruma, major wheel). (b) Vehicle

**Kuzure (v. kuzureru)** To crumble, collapse, break down. Thus a free translation of kuzure-kesa-gatame would be broken scarf hold. A hold that is not quite the basic or pure form (hon); (kuzure-kami-shiho-gatame, broken upper four quarters hold; kuzure-yoko-shiho-gatame, broken side four quarters)

**Kuzushi** Breaking of balance

**Kyu** A judo 'student' grade, represented by a coloured belt

**Ma** Direct, exact, absolutely (Ma-sutemi-waza, direct (to the rear) sacrifice throw)

**Machi-dojo** Street dojo, small local dojo

**Mae** Front

**Maki-komi** Winding, to wrap or roll up, to throw by rolling oneself so that the opponent is 'locked on' to one's body

**Manaka** Centre, 'inside' the contest area

**Ma-sutemi-waza** Technique whereby the attacker (tori) falls straight on to his back to throw

**Mata** The thigh

**Matte** Refereeing word meaning 'wait', or 'break'

**Meijin** Master player, expert

**Mi** Human body

**Migi** Right side

**Mizu** Water

**Mon** Gate, junior grade

**Morote** Both hands (morote-seoi-nage, elbow shoulder throw; morote-gari, double hand grip)

**Mune** Chest (mune-gatame, chest hold)

**Nage (v. nageru)** To throw (nage-waza, throwing techniques; nage-komi, throwing practise)

**Nage-no-kata** Forms of throwing; fifteen selected throws executed both left and right to train the participants in body control and appreciation of judo technique

**Na-me** Wave (of water)

**Nami (v. naruberu)** To place in a line, range in a row

**Ne (v. neru)** To lie down

**Ne-waza** Technique carried out on the ground in a lying position

**Nige-waza (v. nigeru)** Escape technique (usually in groundwork)

**No** Belonging to. A link word as in nage-no-kata

**O** Big, large, major (o-uchi-gari, major inner reaping)

**Obi** Belt

**Ogoshi** Major hip

**Ogurama** Major wheel

**Okii** Big

**Okuri (v. okuru)** To send forward (okuri-eri-jime, sliding lapel neck-lock)

**Okuri-ashi-harai** Sweeping ankle through

**Omoi** Heavy

**Osae-komi** Holding (osae-komi-waza, holding technique/s); referees' call signalling that a hold is effective

**Oshi (v. osu)** To push

**Osoto-gari** Major outer reaping

**Osoto-guruma** Major outer wheel

**Otoshi (v. otosu)** To drop (tai-otoshi, body drop)

**O-uchi-gake** Major driving

**Owari** The end

**Randori** Free practise

**Rei** Bow

**Renraku** Connection, communication, contact

**Renraku-waza** Combination technique

**Renshu** To practise

**Renzoku-waza** Comprehensive name for techniques linked up in any way

**Ritsu-rei** As with tachi-rei meaning 'standing bow'

**Ronin** An unretained samurai warrior

**Ryote** Two hands

**Ryu** School. Attached to most of the names of the old ju-jitsu systems (e.g. Kito-ryu)

**Saikatanden** The lower abdomen

**Samurai** A knight of feudal Japan (a social class), *see* bushi

**Sangaku** Turnover

**Sangaku-jime** Triangular strangle

**Sesae** To support, prop (sasae-tsuri-komi-ashi, propping drawing ankle)

**Sei-ryoku-senyo** The principle of maximum efficiency in the use of mind and body

**Senaka** The back (of a body)

**Sensei** Teacher, master

**Senshu** A competitor, champion

**Seoi (v. seou)** To carry on the back (translated into English seoi-nage is more commonly known as shoulder throw)

**Seoi-otoshi** A mixture of shoulder throw and body drop

**Seppuku** The bushi method of committing suicide. Normally erroneously called Harai-kiri

**Shiai** Contest

**Shiai-jo** Contest area

**Shido** Note (penalty equivalent to three points)

**Shihan** Master, past-master

**Shiho** Four quarters, four directions

**Shiki** Style, ceremony

**Shime (jime) (v. shimeru)** To tighten, strangle

**Shime-waza** Technique of strangling

**Shimoza** 'Lower seat', the ordinary members' side of the dojo

**Shisei** Posture

**Shita** Below, underneath

**Shizen** Nature

**Shizentai** Natural (upright) posture

**Sode** Sleeve

**Sogo-gachi** Compound win by ippon made up of a score of waza-ari added to the benefit of a keikoku penalty

**Sona-mama** Freeze (referees' instruction)

**Sore-made** That's all, finish (referees' command)

**Soto** Outside, outer (osoto-gari, major outer reaping)

**Soto-makikomi** Winding throw

**Sukui (v. sukuku)** To scoop up

**Sumi** Corner

**Sumi-gaeshi** Corner throw

**Sutemi (v. suteru)** To throw away

**Sutemi-waza** Technique whereby the attacker throws away his own body, sacrifices his own posture

**Tachi (v. Tatsu)** To stand

**Tachi-rei** Standing bow

**Tachi-waza** Technique performed in a standing position, standing practise

**Tai** Body

**Tai-sabaki** Body movement

**Taiso** Physical exercise

**Tani** Valley (tani-otoshi, valley drop)

**Tatami** Rice-straw mats used in dojos and Japanese houses

**Tate** Vertical (tate-shiho-gatama, vertical four quarters hold)

**Te** Hand (te-waza, hand techniques; te-garuma, hand throw)

**Tekubi** Wrist

**Tokeka** Hold broken. A command given by the referee to indicate the 'count must stop' when a contestant has effectively broken the hold by which he was being secured

**Tokui** Favourite, special (tokui-waza, favourite technique)

**Tomoe** Turning over, twisting over, whirling over (tomoe-nage, stomach throw)

**Tori (v. toru)** (a) The name used often in technical explanation for the person who applies the technique. (b) To grasp, to hold in the hands

**Tsuki-waza** Poke, stab, thrust or punch technique

**Tsugi-ashi** A manner of walking in which one foot leads at each step and the other never passes it

**Tsuri** To 'fish' up (tsuri-komi, lift up and pull forward; tsuri-goshi, fishing hip)

**Tsurikomi-goshi** Drawing hip

**Tsuyoi** Strong

**Uchi-komi (v. utsukomu)** To beat against, to go in. A repetitive exercise where the throwing technique is taken to the point of kake

**Uchi-mata** Inner thigh throw

**Ude** Arm (ude-gatame, straight armlock; ude-garami, bent armlock)

**Ue** Above, on top of

**Uke (v. ukeru)** To receive. The name used often in technical explanations for the person on whom the technique is applied

**Ukemi** Breakfall

**Uki (v. uku)** To float, buoyant (uki-goshi, floating hip; uki-otoshi, floating drop)

**Uki-waza** Floating technique

**Ura** Back, rear (ura-nage, rear throw)

**Ushira** Behind, back of (ushiro-jime, any strangle from behind)

**Utsuri (v. utsuru)** To change, to move (utsuri-goshi, changing hip)

**Wakare (v. wakareru)** To divide, separate (yoko-wakare, side separation)

**Waza** Technique

**Waza-ari** A score, almost an ippon (value seven points)

**Waza-ari awasete ippon** Ippon achieved by having scored two waza-ari

**Yama** Mountain (yama-arashi, mountain storm)

**Yoko** Side (yoko-shiho-gatame, side four quarters hold; yoko-tome-nage, side stomach throw)

**Yoko-gake** Side hook

**Yoko-otoshi** Side drop

**Yoko-wakare** Side parting

**Yoshi** Let's go, let's get on with it. Referee's command used after sona-mama

**Yowai** Weak

**Yubi** Finger, or toe if used as in ashi-no-yubi

**Yuko** A score, almost a waza-ari (five points)

**Yusei-gachi** A win by superiority

**Za-rei** Formal kneeling bow

**Za-zen** Kneeling motionless in concentrated force, meditation

**Zori** Toe-grip straw sandals used by judoka when in judo-gi moving to and from the mat edge

# WHERE TO LEARN

To find out more about how to start judo, and for a list of clubs in your area, write to:

**THE BRITISH JUDO ASSOCIATION**
**16 Upper Woburn Place**
**London WC1H 0QH**

**I would like to dedicate this book to my wife, Alison, and son Ashley**

## Acknowledgements

An extra special thank you to Alison, whose help on the book has been invaluable, and to Arlene, my mother-in-law, for helping with the typing.

I would also like to thank Angelo Parisi, Karen Briggs, Ray Stevens, Edward Ferry and Ingrid Berghmans for their help with the photographs.

First published 1988 by Pan Books Ltd, Cavaye Place, London SW10 9PG
9 8 7 6 5 4 3 2 1
Text © Neil Adams MBE 1988
Photographs © Dave Finch 1988
Designer: John Hawkins

ISBN 0 330 30140 3

Photoset by Parker Typesetting Service, Leicester
Printed by Richard Clay Ltd, Bungay, Suffolk